LE CREUSET®

ONE-POT CUISINE

LE CREUSET®

ONE-POT CUISINE

CLASSIC RECIPES FOR CASSEROLES, TAGINES & SIMPLE ONE-POT DISHES

MITCHELL BEAZLEY

CONTENTS

A KITCHEN CLASSIC

For almost 100 years, from the company's foundry in Fresnoy-Le-Grand, Northern France, Le Creuset cookware has been created from the finest materials. The French brand has stood for the best quality in the kitchen for generations, used by top chefs and keen home cooks the world over.

Each item of Le Creuset cast iron cookware is individually hand-crafted to ensure uncompromising quality and durability. Molten iron is poured into moulds to cast the shape, then cooled. Once cooled, the pot is removed from the mould and each mould is broken and recycled, meaning no two pieces of Le Creuset cookware are ever exactly the same. Each piece is then passed through the hands of 15 different skilled craftsmen in a meticulous 12-step finishing process, to be cleaned and smoothed, ready for enamelling. The enamel provides a highly durable, hygienic and shock-resistant finish.

Given the attention to detail devoted to the production process, it is no wonder that a Le Creuset pot, pan or grill can be found in the kitchens of discerning home cooks everywhere, in large country houses, contemporary apartments and bustling family homes. Reflecting an international popularity, Le Creuset products now include the cast iron Tatin dish, the cast iron Balti dish, the Stoneware Tapas dish and the cast iron Wok. From the trademark Volcanic orange to the more muted Chiffon Pink, classic Flint to bright Teal, everyone has their preferred colour. With their flawless craftsmanship and classic style, Le Creuset products are owned with pride and affection.

So what better way to prepare delicious one-pot meals than in Le Creuset cookware? Exclusively created for the brand's famous cast iron pots, tagines and grill pans, this book is bursting with more than 100 mouth-watering recipes for wonderful casseroles, tagines and simple one-pot suppers. From slow-cooked, hearty stews to divine desserts, food for sharing on a warm, sunny day to aromatic and flavoursome tagines for an autumnal evening, there is a recipe here for every occasion.

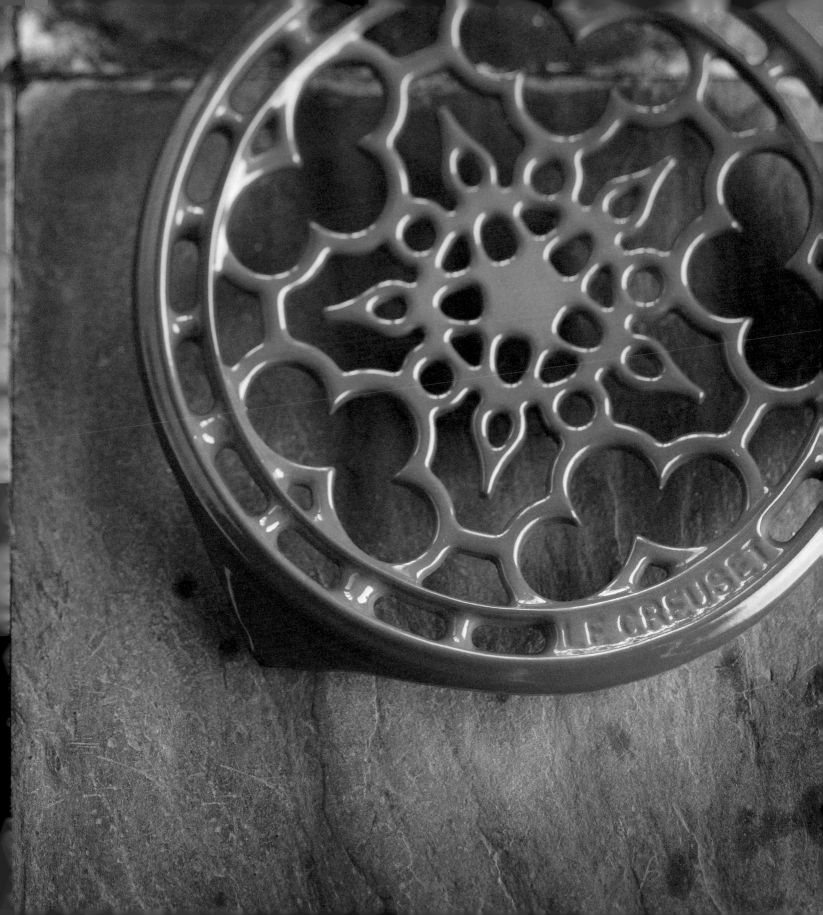

MEAT

24cm Round Casserole

A CLASSIC BEEF CASSEROLE
Enjoy this warming casserole in the cold winter months.

SERVES 4–6
Prep time: 15 minutes
Cooking time: 2 hours 15 minutes

2 tablespoons olive oil

800g stewing beef,
cut into 4cm cubes

2 large onions, cut into large pieces

4 carrots, cut into large pieces

1 parsnip, cut into large pieces

1 Granny Smith apple, peeled,
cored and cut into 1cm dice

2 garlic cloves, finely chopped

2 tablespoons tomato ketchup

1 tablespoon soft light brown sugar

1 tablespoon cider vinegar

3 thyme sprigs

2 bay leaves

330ml dark ale

100ml beef stock

2 tablespoons wholegrain mustard

1 slice of wholemeal bread

1 tablespoon cornflour (optional)

Salt and freshly ground black pepper

Heat the oil in the casserole over a medium heat, add the beef and cook until browned on all sides.

Add the onions and fry for 2–3 minutes. Add the carrots and parsnip, season with salt and pepper and continue to cook for 3–4 minutes until the onions are soft.

Add the apple, garlic, tomato ketchup, sugar, vinegar, thyme and bay leaves, stir, then pour in the ale. Cook for 2 minutes, stirring to remove any browned bits stuck to the bottom of the casserole. Pour in the stock and bring to a simmer.

Spread the mustard over one side of the bread and place it on top of the casserole, mustard side down. Cover with the lid and cook over a low heat for 1½–2 hours until the beef is tender. If you prefer a thicker sauce, thicken the gravy by mixing the cornflour with a little water. Stir it into the casserole towards the end of the cooking time and cook for a further 5 minutes until thickened.

24cm Round Casserole

SERVES 4–6
Prep time: 20 minutes
Cooking time: 2 hours 15 minutes

POT-AU-FEU MAISON
A century-old French recipe with an Italian twist.

For the gremolata:

1 garlic clove, finely chopped

1 handful of flat-leaf parsley, chopped

Finely grated zest of 1 lemon

For the casserole:

1 tablespoon butter

1 tablespoon olive oil

800g stewing beef, cut into 4cm cubes

1 tablespoon plain flour

1 onion, chopped

2 bouquets garni

3 parsnips, cubed

4 carrots, cubed

½ small butternut squash, deseeded and cubed (optional)

400g potatoes, cubed

100g Brussels sprouts

200ml white wine

280ml beef stock

1 garlic clove, crushed

Salt and freshly ground black pepper

Preheat the oven to 180°C.

For the gremolata, mix together all the ingredients and set to one side.

Melt the butter and oil in the casserole over a medium heat. Dust the beef in the flour until coated, then add the meat to the casserole and cook until browned on all sides. Add the onion and bouquets garni and fry for 3–4 minutes until the onion is softened.

Add the prepared vegetables, wine, stock and garlic to the casserole and stir until combined. Season with salt and pepper. Bring the contents to a simmer and cover with the lid.

Place the casserole in the oven for 1½–2 hours until the beef is tender and starting to fall apart.

Serve the stew sprinkled with the gremolata.

Reversible Grill Pan

GINGER-SOY CHARGRILLED STEAK

A fragrant, Asian-inspired simple meal.

SERVES 6

Prep time: 20 minutes, plus marinating
Cooking time: 10 minutes

---

3 steaks, about 400g each

Olive oil, for greasing

Freshly ground black pepper

A few coriander sprigs, to garnish

For the ginger-soy marinade:

5cm piece fresh root ginger, peeled and thinly sliced

3 garlic cloves, thinly sliced

200ml light soy sauce

2 tablespoons sesame oil

1½ tablespoons mirin

1 teaspoon sugar

For the Asian salad:

3 large carrots, halved and cut into long, thin strips

1 cucumber, quartered, deseeded and cut into long, thin strips

100g bean sprouts

Mix together all the ingredients for the ginger-soy marinade in a bowl. Set aside 2 tablespoons of the marinade to make a dressing for the Asian salad.

Season the steaks with pepper and place them in a large, non-metallic dish. Pour over the marinade and leave to marinate, covered, for at least 1 hour, turning the steaks occasionally.

For the Asian salad, combine the carrots, cucumber and bean sprouts in a bowl and spoon over the reserved ginger-soy marinade.

Remove the steaks from the marinade, allowing any excess to drip off. Heat the grill pan over a high heat and grease it with oil. Place the steaks on the grill and cook for 3–5 minutes on each side, or until cooked to your liking. Remove from the pan, cover with foil, and leave to rest for 5 minutes.

Halve each steak and serve with any pan juices spooned over, with the Asian salad. Garnish with coriander before serving.

26cm Round Casserole

SERVES 4–6
Prep time: 15 minutes
Cooking time: 4 hours 45 minutes

ORIENTAL-SPICED BEEF
An aromatic spiced broth transforms this beef stew into something special.

3 tablespoons olive oil

1kg joint of beef for pot-roasting

3 litres beef stock

1 onion, chopped

3 lemon grass stalks

6 star anise

2 cinnamon sticks

1–2 mild red chillies

5cm piece fresh root ginger, peeled and thinly sliced

1 tablespoon whole black peppercorns

4 cloves

1 tablespoon sugar

2 tablespoons soy sauce

1 tablespoon fish sauce

200g cooked rice noodles

1 handful of coriander, leaves roughly chopped

125g bean sprouts

125g small shiitake mushrooms, finely chopped

3 spring onions, chopped

2 limes, cut into wedges

Heat the oil in the casserole over a medium heat, add the beef joint and cook until browned on all sides, then remove it from the casserole and set aside. Add the stock to the casserole, stirring to remove any brown bits stuck to the bottom, bring to a simmer and return the beef.

Add the onion, lemon grass, star anise, cinnamon sticks, chillies and ginger. Place the peppercorns and cloves in an infuser or tie in a small piece of muslin and add to the casserole. Stir in the sugar, soy sauce and fish sauce. Cover with the lid and simmer over a low heat for 4–4½ hours until the beef is tender. If needed, add extra soy sauce, to taste, at the end of the cooking time.

Remove the spices and slice the beef. Place the rice noodles, half of the coriander, bean sprouts, shiitake mushrooms and spring onions in serving bowls. Top with the sliced beef and spoon over the broth.

Sprinkle with the remaining coriander and add a squeeze of lime juice.

27cm Tagine

VEAL WITH BROAD BEANS & MINT

This springtime tagine is fresh, vibrant and light.

SERVES 4
Prep time: 15 minutes
Cooking time: 1 hour 45 minutes

2 tablespoons olive oil

800g leg of veal, cut into 4 pieces

2 small onions, finely chopped

175ml water

1 teaspoon ground cumin

1 bunch of flat-leaf parsley, tied together with kitchen string

500g broad beans, shelled

3 mint sprigs, leaves chopped

Salt and freshly ground black pepper

Heat the oil in the tagine base over a medium heat, add the veal and cook until browned on all sides. Add the onions and fry for 5 minutes until soft.

Add the measured water, cumin and parsley and season with salt and pepper. Bring to a simmer, reduce the heat to low, and cover with the lid. Cook the veal for 1½ hours, or until tender.

Stir the broad beans into the tagine with half of the mint. Replace the lid and simmer gently for another 10 minutes or until the beans are cooked.

Serve the tagine sprinkled with the remaining mint.

NOTE: *If you want to remove the outer shell from the broad beans, blanche them first, then drain and immerse in ice-cold water to stop them cooking further. Squeeze the beans out of their grey outer shell and set them aside until needed. Add the beans 5 minutes before the end of the cooking time.*

24cm Oval Cast Iron Dish

SERVES 4
Prep time: 10 minutes
Cooking time: 25 minutes

VEAL CUTLETS WITH TOMATO & MOZZARELLA

The fragrant flavours of Italy on a plate.

8 tomatoes

1 teaspoon olive oil

4 veal cutlets

2 onions, finely chopped

1 garlic clove, finely chopped

4 sage leaves

250g mozzarella cheese, drained and sliced

Salt and freshly ground black pepper

Preheat the oven to 170°C.

To skin the tomatoes, put them in a bowl and pour boiling water over to cover. Leave for 1–2 minutes, then drain, cut a cross at the stem end of each tomato and peel off the skins. Cut the tomatoes into thick slices.

Heat the oil in the ovenproof dish over a medium heat, add the veal cutlets and cook briefly until browned on each side. Remove from the dish, season with salt and pepper, and keep warm.

Turn the heat to low, add the onions and garlic to the dish and fry for 5 minutes until soft, then move to one side of the dish.

Lay the tomatoes in the dish, and place a veal cutlet on each. Spoon the onions and garlic on top, and add a sage leaf to each cutlet. Season with salt and pepper and finish with the mozzarella.

Place the dish in the oven for 20 minutes, or until the mozzarella melts and starts to turn golden.

Serve with pasta, if you like, cooked al dente.

24cm Round Casserole

SERVES 6
Prep time: 20 minutes
Cooking time: 1 hour 45 minutes

CREAMY VEAL RAGOUT

A delicious classic recipe of veal, served two ways, in a creamy sauce.

500g veal, cut into 4cm cubes

3 carrots, sliced

2 onions, chopped

2 leeks, sliced

3 celery sticks, sliced

20 silverskin onions or
small shallots, peeled

20 button mushrooms, cut in half

1 bouquet garni

2–3 cloves

200ml veal or light beef stock

2 tablespoons butter

3 tablespoons flour

200ml double cream

2 egg yolks

Juice of ½ lemon

Salt and freshly ground black pepper

1 small bunch of flat-leaf parsley,
leaves roughly chopped, to garnish

For the meatballs:

250g minced veal

1 egg, lightly beaten

2 tablespoons fresh breadcrumbs

3 flat-leaf parsley sprigs,
leaves finely chopped

2 tablespoons vegetable oil

For the meatballs, mix the minced veal with the egg, breadcrumbs and chopped parsley. With wet hands, form the mince mixture into walnut-sized meatballs and set to one side.

Heat 1 tablespoon of the oil in the casserole over a medium heat, add the meatballs and cook until browned all over, then remove with a slotted spoon and set to one side.

For the casserole, add the remaining oil and the cubed veal to the casserole and cook until browned on all sides, then remove with slotted spoon.

Add the carrots, onions, leeks, celery, onions or shallots, mushrooms, bouquet garni and cloves and fry for 5 minutes until the vegetables are softened.

Return the meatballs and veal to the casserole and pour in the stock. Add enough water to cover and bring to the boil. Reduce the heat to low, cover with the lid, and simmer gently for 1–1¼ hours until the meat is tender. Remove the meatballs, veal and vegetables from the casserole using a slotted spoon, cover and leave to one side. Strain the stock into a jug and set to one side.

Melt the butter in the casserole. Add the flour and cook, stirring, for 1 minute. Pour in the stock, a little at a time, stirring constantly. Bring to a simmer and cook the sauce for 5 minutes until smooth and thickened. Mix together the cream and egg yolks and stir into the sauce.

Return the meatballs, veal and vegetables to the sauce and heat through gently, stirring, then add the lemon juice and season with salt and pepper.

Garnish with parsley and serve with crusty bread or brown rice.

24cm Round Casserole

SERVES 6
Prep time: 25 minutes
Cooking time: 40 minutes

LEBANESE-STYLE MEATBALLS
Meatballs with fresh mint in an aromatic spiced tomato sauce.

For the meatballs:

250g minced beef

250g minced pork

½ small onion, finely chopped

3 tablespoons fresh white breadcrumbs

1 egg, lightly beaten

1 tablespoon finely chopped mint leaves

A pinch of cayenne pepper

½ teaspoon salt

½ teaspoon freshly ground black pepper

2–3 tablespoons flour

½ tablespoon butter

4 tablespoons olive oil

For the tomato sauce:

1 small red onion, finely chopped

2 garlic cloves, crushed

2 x 400g cans chopped tomatoes

1 tablespoon balsamic vinegar

1 teaspoon paprika

½ teaspoon ground cinnamon

½ teaspoon ground cloves

1 teaspoon sugar

100g sun-dried tomatoes, chopped

15g goats' cheese, crumbled

2 teaspoons tomato purée

Salt and freshly ground black pepper

Basil leaves, to garnish

For the meatballs, combine the minced beef and pork with the onion, breadcrumbs, egg, mint, cayenne, salt and pepper. Dust your hands in flour and form the mince mixture into walnut-sized meatballs.

Melt the butter and half of the oil in the casserole over a medium heat and fry the meatballs until browned all over, then remove them from the casserole with a slotted spoon and leave to one side.

To make the tomato sauce, heat the remaining oil in the casserole over a medium heat, add the red onion and garlic and fry for 3 minutes until soft.

Add the tomatoes, vinegar, paprika, cinnamon, cloves and sugar. Season with salt and pepper. Cover the casserole with the lid and cook over a low heat for 15 minutes, stirring regularly.

Stir the sun-dried tomatoes, goats' cheese, tomato purée and browned meatballs into the sauce. Simmer over a medium-low heat for 10–15 minutes, stirring occasionally, until the sauce has reduced and thickened.

Sprinkle with basil leaves and serve with pasta, if liked.

23cm Square Ceramic Dish

SERVES 4
Prep time: 15 minutes
Cooking time: 30 minutes

BAKED MEATBALLS WITH CHERRY SAUCE
Baked in the oven until golden, these meatballs are served with a fruity dark cherry sauce.

400g minced veal

400g minced pork

1 shallot, finely chopped

1 small handful of flat-leaf parsley, leaves chopped

2 eggs

2 tablespoons breadcrumbs

20g butter

2 thyme sprigs

Salt and freshly ground black pepper

For the cherry sauce:

175g frozen, pitted dark cherries

2 tablespoons water

2 teaspoons caster sugar

1½ teaspoons cornflour

Preheat the oven to 175°C.

Mix together the minced veal and pork, shallot, parsley, eggs and breadcrumbs. Season with salt and pepper. With wet hands, form the mince mixture into walnut-sized meatballs.

Grease the ovenproof dish with the butter and add the meatballs in an even layer and top with the thyme. Bake the meatballs for 30 minutes until golden and cooked through. Check regularly, turning the meatballs and spooning over any juices in the bottom of the dish.

To make the cherry sauce, put the frozen cherries and measured water in a microwaveable bowl and cook on high for 2–3 minutes, or until defrosted and heated through. Remove the bowl from the microwave and add the sugar. Mix the cornflour into a splash of hot water and stir it into the cherries until everything is combined. Return the bowl to the microwave for another 1–2 minutes until heated through and thickened. Remove from the microwave and stir well, adding a splash more water if needed. Crush the cherries with the back of a fork to make a smoother sauce, if liked.

Serve the meatballs with the cherry sauce on the side.

**Square Grill Pan
with Double Handles**

PORK CHOPS IN ROSÉ WITH ROSEMARY & ANCHOVIES

This dish captures the aromas and flavours of the south of France.

SERVES 6
Prep time: 10 minutes, plus marinating
Cooking time: 10 minutes

6–8 canned anchovy fillets, drained

3 garlic cloves

Needles from 2 rosemary sprigs

3 tablespoons olive oil

150ml rosé

6 pork chops, about 250g each

Salt and freshly ground black pepper

Mash the anchovies with the garlic, rosemary needles and a little salt and pepper into a coarse paste. Add the oil and rosé and stir until combined.

Place the pork chops in a non-metallic dish and spoon over the marinade. Leave to marinate, covered, in the refrigerator for 3 hours, turning the chops occasionally. Remove the pork from the refrigerator 30 minutes before cooking.

Heat the grill pan over a high heat. Grill the pork chops for 5 minutes on each side, or until cooked to your liking. (You will have to cook the pork in two batches.) Remove the pork from the pan to a warm plate, cover with foil, and leave to rest for 10 minutes.

The pork is delicious served with mashed potatoes and green beans.

27cm Tagine

HERB-STUFFED PORK BELLY

Pork stuffed with fragrant herbs and cooked in a tagine with white wine.

SERVES 6
Prep time: 15 minutes
Cooking time: 1 hour 15 minutes

1.2kg belly pork, rind removed

1 tablespoon thyme, chopped

1 tablespoon rosemary, chopped

1 tablespoon sage, chopped

1 bunch of flat-leaf parsley, leaves chopped

2 tablespoons olive oil

3 shallots, finely chopped

3 garlic cloves, chopped

200ml dry white wine

2 bay leaves

1kg pre-cooked Swiss chard

Light soy sauce to taste

Salt and freshly ground black pepper

Season the pork all over with salt and pepper. Spread the chopped thyme, rosemary, sage and parsley over the underside of the pork belly and roll it up to enclose the herbs. Secure the joint with kitchen string; tie in several places with butcher's knots.

Heat 1 tablespoon of the oil in the tagine base over a medium heat, add the pork joint and cook until browned on all sides. Remove the pork and set to one side.

Add the remaining oil to the tagine and fry the shallots and garlic for 3–5 minutes until soft.

Pour in the white wine, add the bay leaves and simmer gently for 2–3 minutes. Reduce the heat to very low, place the rolled pork in the tagine, cover with the lid, and cook for 1 hour, or until the pork is tender.

Add the cooked chard to the tagine, along with a good splash of soy sauce. Continue to cook for 20 minutes, checking occasionally that there is enough moisture in the tagine. Add water as required.

Remove the pork, cover with foil, and leave to rest for 5 minutes. Place the rested meat on a board, remove the string and cut into slices.

Return the sliced pork with any juices to the tagine, ready to serve.

PORK FILLET WITH HERB SAUCE

The abundance of fresh herbs gives a flavour boost to this simple pork dish.

27cm or 29cm Oval Casserole

SERVES 6
Prep time: 15 minutes
Cooking time: 50 minutes

2 pork tenderloin fillets, about 375–425g each

2 tablespoons olive oil

4 curry leaf sprigs

4 oregano sprigs

4 rosemary sprigs

4 thyme sprigs

Strips of peel and juice of 1 orange

1 tablespoon butter

For the herb sauce:

400ml beef stock

150ml dry white wine

1 shallot, finely chopped

4 tablespoons chopped mixed herbs, such as curry leaves, oregano, rosemary and thyme

2–3 teaspoons cornflour mixed with 1 tablespoon water

50g ice-cold butter, diced

Salt and freshly ground black pepper

Preheat the oven to 180°C.

Season the pork fillets with salt and pepper. Place the two pork fillets together and secure in several places with kitchen string.

Heat the oil in the casserole over a medium heat, add the pork and cook until browned all over. Remove the pork and leave to one side.

Place the herb sprigs and orange peel in the casserole and arrange the pork fillets on top. Pour over the orange juice and dot the top of the meat with the butter. Cover with the lid and put the casserole in the oven for 30–35 minutes until the meat is cooked through – the timing will depend on the thickness of the meat.

Remove the casserole from the oven, place the pork on a warmed plate, cover with foil, and leave to rest for 10 minutes.

While the pork is resting, prepare the herb sauce. Remove the herbs and orange from the casserole and wipe it clean. Add the beef stock, wine and shallot to the casserole. Bring to the boil, add the chopped herbs, then reduce the heat and simmer until the liquid has reduced by one third.

Strain the herb sauce through a sieve and then return it to the casserole. Place over a low heat, add the cornflour mixture and stir until the sauce has thickened slightly. Stir in the diced butter, season with salt and pepper and pour the sauce into a warmed serving jug.

Place the rested meat on a board, remove the string and cut into slices. To serve, arrange the pork on plates, spoon over any juices and accompany with the herb sauce.

Spring vegetables are the perfect accompaniment to the pork.

27cm Tagine

CHORIZO & CELERIAC ONE-POT

Despite its Spanish influence, this simple one-pot meal of chorizo and celeriac is cooked in a tagine.

SERVES 2–3
Prep time: 15 minutes
Cooking time: 1 hour 10 minutes

2 tablespoons olive oil

2 small red onions, cut into thin rings

500g celeriac, cut into thick slices and halved

200ml water

2 bay leaves

A few thyme sprigs

200g cooking chorizo sausages

Salt and freshly ground black pepper

1 small bunch of flat-leaf parsley, leaves roughly chopped, to garnish

Heat the oil in the tagine base over a medium heat, add the onions and sauté for 10 minutes until lightly caramelized.

Add the celeriac, the measured water, bay leaves and thyme and place the chorizo sausages on top. Reduce the heat to low, cover with the lid and cook for 1 hour, or until the celeriac is tender.

Season with salt and pepper and sprinkle over the parsley just before serving.

**Square Plancha
with Double Handles**

SPANISH CHORIZO WITH EGGS & MANCHEGO

In Spain, Manchego cheese is often served as part of tapas. Here, it is integrated into a wholesome grilled dish.

SERVES 2
Prep time: 15 minutes
Cooking time: 25 minutes

2 peppers (any colour), deseeded and sliced

Olive oil, for brushing

75g spicy chorizo, sliced

1 small red onion, thickly sliced

8 cherry tomatoes, cut in half

2 eggs

½ teaspoon paprika

1 teaspoon Provençal spices

40g Manchego cheese, grated, plus extra to serve

Salt and freshly ground black pepper

Brush the sliced peppers with a little oil. Heat the grill pan over a high heat, lightly grease with oil, add the peppers and grill for 10 minutes, turning once, until starting to blacken.

Turn the heat down to medium, add the chorizo and onion and cook for 5 minutes until the onion starts to colour. Add the cherry tomatoes and cook for 3 minutes until softened slightly. Season with salt and pepper.

Make two holes in the vegetable mixture and crack an egg into each one. Sprinkle with paprika, Provençal spices and the Manchego.

Cover the grill pan with a fitted lid or foil; make sure that the foil does not touch the peppers. Cook for 5–7 minutes over a low heat until the eggs are cooked through. Serve with extra Manchego on the side.

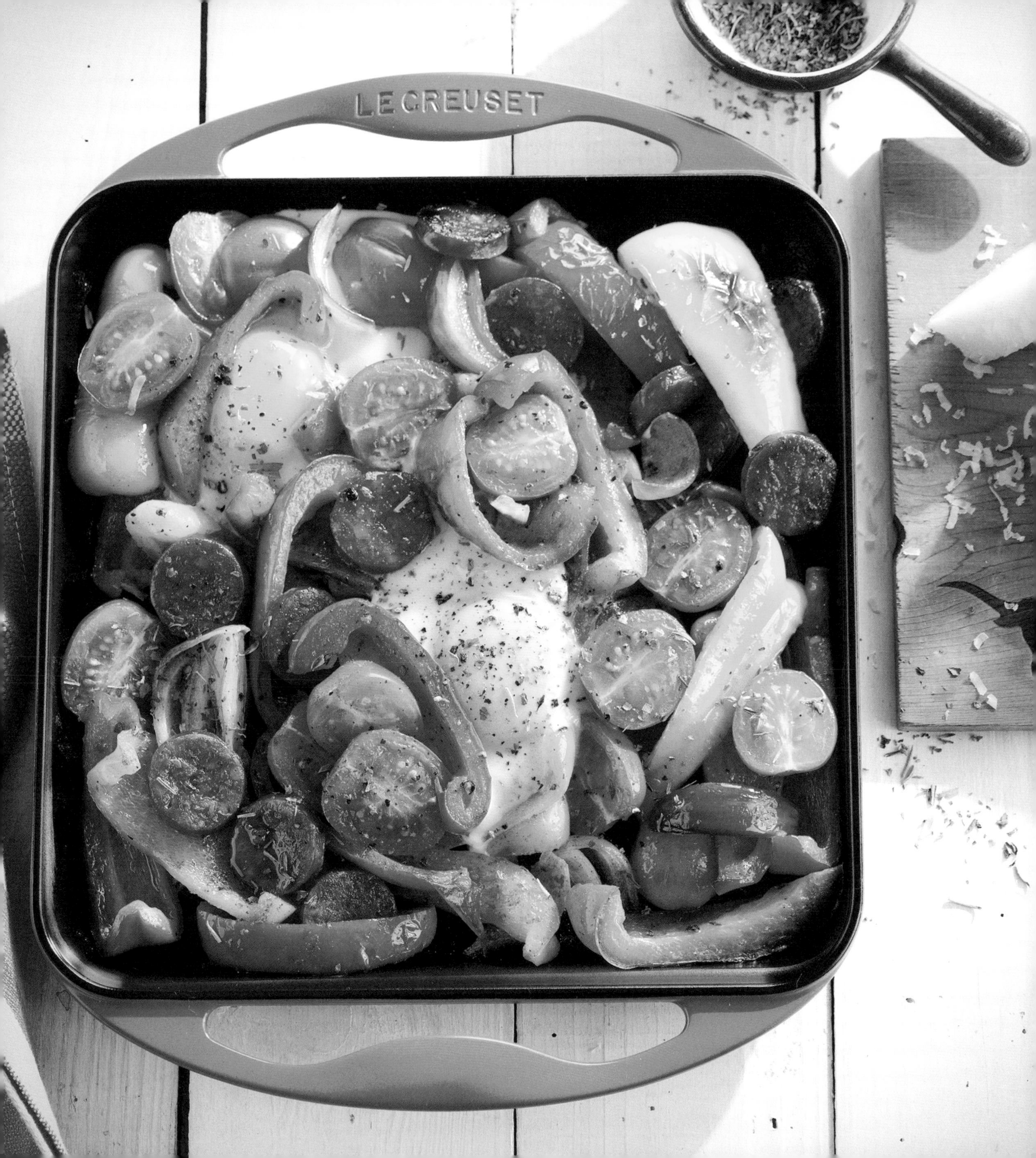
LE CREUSET

MEDITERRANEAN SAUSAGE CASSEROLE

A hearty meal influenced by Mediterranean-style cooking.

22cm or 24cm Casserole

SERVES 4
Prep time: 10 minutes
Cooking time: 45 minutes

1 tablespoon olive oil

8 thick pork sausages, pricked

1 onion, chopped

1 red, green and yellow pepper, deseeded and cut into large pieces

2 celery sticks, roughly diced

2 garlic cloves, crushed

3 thyme sprigs

3 oregano sprigs

1½ teaspoons paprika

½ teaspoon cayenne pepper

1 tablespoon red wine vinegar

1 tablespoon plain flour

700ml chicken stock

1 x 400g can chopped tomatoes

Salt and freshly ground black pepper

Finely chopped spring onions and flat-leaf parsley, to garnish

Heat the oil in the casserole over a medium heat, add the sausages and cook until browned all over. Remove the sausages from the pan and set to one side.

Add the onion, peppers and celery to the casserole and fry for 10–12 minutes until softened. Add the garlic, thyme, oregano and spices and fry for another 2–3 minutes. Add the vinegar and flour and cook, stirring, for 1–2 minutes.

Return the sausages to the casserole. Stir in the chicken stock, chopped tomatoes and season with salt and pepper. Bring to a simmer and cook for 15 minutes until the sauce has reduced and thickened.

Serve the casserole with a sprinkling of spring onions and parsley.

Try serving with crusty bread for mopping up the sauce.

SAUSAGES WITH WHITE BEANS, RED PEPPER & SAFFRON
A warming supper dish for the cold winter months.

27cm Tagine

SERVES 4
Prep time: 15 minutes, plus soaking
Cooking time: 3 hours

200g dried white beans, such as cannellini or butter beans

2 large tomatoes

2 tablespoons duck fat

4 thick pork sausages

2 small onions, chopped

125g thick bacon rashers, diced

2 garlic cloves, crushed

½ large red pepper, deseeded and cut into small dice

1 teaspoon mild smoked paprika

A pinch of saffron threads

1 bouquet garni

250ml water, plus extra if needed

Salt and freshly ground black pepper

½ bunch of flat-leaf parsley, leaves roughly chopped, to garnish

Place the beans in a large bowl, cover with cold water, and leave to soak overnight. Drain and rinse the beans.

To skin the tomatoes, put them in a bowl and pour over boiling water to cover. Leave for 1–2 minutes, then drain, cut a cross at the stem end of each tomato and peel off the skins. Dice the tomatoes and leave to one side.

Heat 1 tablespoon of the duck fat in the tagine base over a medium heat, add the sausages and cook until browned all over. Remove the sausages and set to one side.

Add the remaining duck fat to the tagine base and fry the onions and bacon, stirring occasionally, for 10 minutes, or until lightly golden. Add the garlic, red pepper, diced tomatoes, paprika and saffron and stir well. Reduce the heat to low, cover with the lid and cook for 10 minutes.

Stir the white beans, bouquet garni and the measured water into the sauce. Reduce the heat to very low, replace the lid and cook for 2½ hours, or until the beans are tender. Check occasionally to see if there is enough moisture in the tagine and, if needed, add extra water as required.

Season with salt and pepper and stir in the browned sausages. Replace the lid and cook gently for a further 20 minutes, or until the sausages are cooked through. Sprinkle parsley over the tagine before serving.

24cm Round Casserole

SERVES 6
Prep time: 15 minutes
Cooking time: 40 minutes

CASSOULET
Bring the Pyrenees to your home with this rich and hearty cassoulet.

3 tomatoes

½ tablespoon vegetable oil

250g gammon, cut into pieces

250g sausages, pricked

100g smoked sausage, skin removed and sliced

2 onions, chopped

2 garlic cloves, crushed

1 x 400g can white beans, drained

1 x 200g can kidney beans, drained

1 x 230g can butter beans, drained

100ml dry white wine

2 bay leaves

4 cloves

2 tablespoons tomato purée

2 teaspoons mustard

1 tablespoon molasses

Salt and freshly ground black pepper

To skin the tomatoes, put them in a bowl and pour over boiling water to cover. Leave for 1–2 minutes, then drain, cut a cross at the stem end of each tomato and peel off the skins. Dice the tomatoes and leave to one side.

Heat the oil in the casserole over a medium heat, add the gammon, sausages and smoked sausage and cook until browned all over. Season the meat with pepper, then remove it from the casserole and set to one side.

Add the onions and garlic to the casserole and fry for 2–3 minutes until lightly coloured. Stir in the diced tomatoes along with the beans, wine, bay leaves, cloves, tomato purée, mustard and molasses. Return the meat to the casserole and bring to a simmer. Cover with the lid and cook over a low heat for 20 minutes.

Take the casserole out of the oven and remove the bay leaves and cloves, ready to serve.

24cm Round Casserole

SERVES 4
Prep time: 15 minutes
Cooking time: 1 hour 45 minutes

PORK CHEEKS IN DARK ALE

Here, this cheap cut of pork is turned into something special.

40g butter

250g mushrooms, cut into quarters

1 tablespoon olive oil

800g pork cheeks, trimmed

2 onions, chopped

1 tablespoon flour

200ml dark ale

100ml beef stock

1 thyme sprig

2 bay leaves

Salt and freshly ground black pepper

Preheat the oven to 175°C.

Heat half the butter over a medium heat, add the mushrooms and fry for 8 minutes until starting to brown and there is no trace of liquid in the casserole. Remove with a slotted spoon and leave to one side.

Heat the remaining butter and the oil in the casserole over a medium heat, add the pork cheeks and cook until browned all over. Remove from the casserole and set to one side.

Add the onions and fry until lightly caramelized, then season with salt and pepper. Stir in the flour and cook for 1 minute, then add the ale, stock, thyme and bay leaves. Return the pork cheeks and stir until combined.

Cover with the lid – or, if desired, transfer to a ceramic dish (as shown) and cover with foil – and place in the oven for 1½ hours, or until the pork cheeks are tender. Stir the mushrooms into the casserole for the last 5 minutes of cooking and warm through.

Delicious served Belgian-style with freshly cooked chips.

27cm Tagine

SERVES 4
Prep time: 15 minutes, plus soaking
Cooking time: 2 hours 30 minutes

LAMB WITH APRICOTS, RAISINS & CHICKPEAS

A lightly spiced lamb tagine with fruit, chickpeas and fresh coriander.

125g dried chickpeas

1 tablespoon olive oil

600g boned lamb leg or shoulder meat, cut into 2.5cm cubes

2 onions, chopped

A generous pinch of saffron threads

¼ teaspoon ground ginger

⅓ cinnamon stick

250ml water, plus extra if needed

200g fresh apricots, pitted and cut in half (or 8 dried apricots, cut in half)

35g raisins

1 teaspoon honey

1 small bunch of coriander, leaves roughly chopped

Salt and freshly ground black pepper

Place the beans in a large bowl, cover with cold water and leave to soak overnight. Drain and rinse the beans.

Heat the oil in the tagine base over a medium heat, add the lamb and cook until browned on all sides. Remove the lamb with a slotted spoon and set to one side.

Add the onions to the tagine base and fry until lightly caramelized.

Return the browned lamb to the tagine, stir in the saffron, ginger, cinnamon stick and the drained chickpeas and pour over the measured water. Bring to a simmer then reduce the heat to low, cover with the lid and cook for 2 hours, or until the lamb and chickpeas are tender. Check occasionally that there is enough moisture in the tagine and, if necessary, add some extra water.

Stir the apricots, raisins, honey and half of the coriander leaves into the tagine. Season with salt and pepper. (Only add salt once the chickpeas are cooked.) Continue to cook over a low heat with the lid on for 20 minutes.

Serve the tagine with the remaining coriander sprinkled over.

30cm Shallow Casserole

SERVES 4

Prep time: 20 minutes
Cooking time: 1 hour 10 minutes

LAMB NAVARIN

A lightly spiced version of the classic, slow-cooked French casserole.

1 tablespoon butter

2 tablespoons olive oil

800g boned lamb shoulder or neck meat, cut into 2.5cm cubes

½ teaspoon salt

1 teaspoon black pepper

1 tablespoon plain flour

200ml light ale with a squeeze of lemon, or lemon Belgian beer

1 shallot, finely chopped

2 garlic cloves, crushed

25g piece fresh root ginger, peeled and finely chopped

2 carrots, cut into 2cm dice

200g fine green beans, trimmed

300g canned chickpeas, drained

200ml vegetable stock

2 teaspoons ground coriander

2 teaspoons ground cumin

2 teaspoons caraway seeds

½ teaspoon ground cinnamon

A pinch of saffron threads

1 tablespoon honey

Salt and freshly ground black pepper

5 tablespoons roughly chopped mint, to garnish

5 tablespoons roughly chopped coriander, to garnish

Heat the butter and oil in the casserole over a medium heat, add the lamb and cook until browned on all sides. Stir in the salt and pepper.

Sprinkle over the flour and cook, stirring, for 1 minute. Pour in the ale or beer, stir to remove any brown bits stuck to the bottom of the casserole and cook until reduced.

Add the shallot, garlic, ginger, carrots and green beans to the casserole. Stir in the chickpeas, vegetable stock and spices. Cover with the lid and cook slowly for 45 minutes–1 hour, stirring occasionally, until the lamb is tender.

Stir in the honey and season to taste. Just before serving, sprinkle over the fresh herbs.

You could serve this dish with toasted pitta bread.

27cm Tagine

LAMB KEFTA IN TOMATO SAUCE WITH BAKED EGGS

Aromatic spiced meatballs with eggs and cooked in a fresh tomato sauce.

SERVES 4
Prep time: 20 minutes
Cooking time: 55 minutes

For the lamb kefta:

500g lean minced lamb

1 large onion, chopped

½ bunch of coriander, leaves chopped, plus extra to garnish

6 mint leaves, chopped

1 teaspoon mild chilli powder

A pinch of allspice

A pinch of ground cinnamon

½ teaspoon ground cumin

2 tablespoons olive oil

For the tagine:

250g fresh tomatoes

½ teaspoon ground ginger

½ teaspoon ground cumin

½ bunch of flat-leaf parsley, leaves chopped

100ml water

4 eggs

Salt and freshly ground black pepper

For the lamb kefta, mix the lamb mince with half the chopped onion, the coriander, mint, chilli powder, allspice, cinnamon and cumin. Season with a pinch of salt. With wet hands, form the mince mixture into small balls, roughly 3cm in diameter.

Heat 1 tablespoon of the oil in the tagine base and fry the meatballs until browned on all sides. Remove from the tagine and set to one side.

For the tagine, first skin the tomatoes. Put them in a bowl and pour over boiling water to cover. Leave for 1–2 minutes, then drain, cut a cross at the stem end of each tomato and peel off the skins. Dice the tomatoes and leave to one side.

Heat the remaining oil in the tagine base and fry the reserved half of the chopped onion over a low heat until translucent. Add the diced tomato, ginger, cumin, parsley and the measured water. Bring the sauce to a simmer then reduce the heat to low and cook for 20 minutes. Season to taste with salt and pepper.

Add the meatballs to the sauce, cover with the lid and simmer over a medium-low heat for 20 minutes until cooked through.

Reduce the heat to the lowest temperature, make 4 dips spaced well apart in the sauce and break an egg into each one. Replace the lid and continue to cook for 5 minutes until the eggs are cooked. Garnish with coriander and serve immediately.

29cm Oval Casserole

SERVES 4
Prep time: 15 minutes
Cooking time: 1 hour 20 minutes

LEG OF LAMB WITH LENTILS
Lamb, figs and lentils, a heart-warming combination.

600g boned lamb leg joint

1 tablespoon olive oil

1 tablespoon butter

2 shallots, chopped

1 garlic clove, crushed

1 carrot, finely diced

150ml red wine

300g Puy lentils, rinsed

700ml vegetable stock

2 bay leaves

2–3 fresh sage sprigs

4 fresh figs, cut in half

2–3 flat-leaf parsley sprigs,
leaves chopped

A dash of cider vinegar

Salt and freshly ground
black pepper

Season the lamb with salt and pepper.

Heat the oil and butter in the casserole over a medium heat, add the lamb and cook until browned on all sides. Remove the lamb and cover with foil to keep it warm.

Add the shallots, garlic and carrot and cook in the juices from the meat for 5 minutes, stirring. Pour in the red wine and cook until reduced, stirring to remove any brown bits stuck to the bottom of the pan.

Stir in the lentils, stock, bay leaves and sage, bring to the boil over a medium heat, then reduce the heat and simmer for 10 minutes. Add the browned lamb and the figs. Cover with the lid and cook over a low heat for 40–50 minutes until the lentils and the meat are cooked. Check towards the end of the cooking time and add a little water if the mixture has become too dry.

Take the meat out of the casserole and leave it to rest for 5–10 minutes. Stir the parsley and vinegar into the lentils and season with salt and pepper. Slice the lamb and serve it with the lentils.

LAMB WITH PRUNES, ALMONDS & HONEY

A classic Moroccan tagine, full of flavour.

27cm Tagine

SERVES 6
Prep time: 15 minutes
Cooking time: 2 hours 15 minutes

2 tablespoons olive oil

1.25kg boned lamb leg or shoulder meat, cut into 12 pieces

2 large onions, sliced

1 garlic clove, chopped

A pinch of saffron threads

1 teaspoon ground ginger

2 cinnamon sticks

250ml water, plus extra as required

300g Agen prunes

2 tablespoons honey

½ teaspoon ground cinnamon

20g butter

50g toasted almonds, skins removed

2 tablespoons toasted sesame seeds

Salt and freshly ground black pepper

Heat 1 tablespoon of the oil in the tagine base over a medium heat, add half of the lamb and cook until browned on all sides, then set aside. Repeat with the remaining lamb and set aside.

Add the second tablespoon of oil and the onions to the tagine base and fry until the onions are lightly caramelized.

Stir in the garlic and return the browned pieces of lamb to the tagine. Sprinkle over the saffron and ginger, add the cinnamon sticks and season with salt and pepper.

Add the measured water and bring to the boil, cover with the lid, then reduce the heat to very low and cook for 1 hour. Stir in the prunes, honey, ground cinnamon and butter, cover and cook for a further 1 hour, or until the lamb is tender. Check occasionally that there is enough moisture in the tagine and, if necessary, add extra water as required.

Ten minutes before the end of the cooking time, stir in the toasted almonds and adjust the seasoning to taste. Sprinkle over the toasted sesame seeds and serve.

NOTE: *The tagine base placed over a low heat can be used to toast nuts and seeds.*

POULTRY & GAME

24cm Round Casserole

SERVES 4
Prep time: 15 minutes
Cooking time: 1 hour 45 minutes

COQ AU VIN BLANC
A twist on the classic chicken dish with a rich, creamy white wine sauce.

1kg whole chicken, cut into quarters

1 tablespoon vegetable oil

2 tablespoons butter

50g bacon, cut into 1cm dice

2 shallots, finely chopped

1 garlic clove, finely chopped

250g button mushrooms,
cut into quarters

1 tablespoon plain flour

200ml sherry

500ml dry white wine

3 large tomatoes, deseeded and diced

2 bay leaves

3 thyme sprigs

100ml double cream

Salt and freshly ground black pepper

Season the chicken portions with salt and pepper and set to one side.

Heat the oil and butter in the casserole over a medium heat, add the bacon and fry until golden.

Stir in the shallots, garlic and mushrooms and continue to fry for 3–4 minutes until the vegetables are soft. Remove everything from the casserole with a slotted spoon, leaving the oil behind.

Add the chicken to the hot oil and cook until browned on all sides. Sprinkle over the flour and stir. Pour in the sherry and wine and cook until reduced, stirring to remove any brown bits stuck to the bottom of the casserole. Add the tomatoes, bay leaves and thyme and bring to the boil.

Return the bacon, shallots, garlic and mushrooms to the casserole, then reduce the heat to low, cover with the lid and simmer for 1 hour, stirring occasionally, until the chicken is tender.

Remove the lid from the casserole, take out the bay leaves and cook for a further 30 minutes, adding some water if the sauce is too dry, until the chicken is cooked through. Stir in the cream and warm through just before serving.

NOTE: *Ask your butcher to portion the chicken for you.*

27cm Tagine

SERVES 3
Prep time: 15 minutes
Cooking time: 1 hour 45 minutes

CHICKEN WITH CARAMELIZED APPLES

Succulent spiced chicken with caramelized apples and crunchy sesame seeds.

1 tablespoon olive oil

700g chicken thighs on the bone

2 onions, finely chopped

⅓ teaspoon ground cinnamon

A pinch of saffron threads

1 teaspoon ground ginger

1 bunch of coriander, leaves chopped

150ml water, plus extra as required

Salt and freshly ground black pepper

2 tablespoons toasted sesame seeds, to garnish

For the caramelized apples:

3 Braeburn apples, peeled, cored and thickly sliced

2 teaspoons honey

30g salted butter

1 small cinnamon stick

¼ teaspoon nutmeg

For the caramelized apples, place the apples, honey, butter, cinnamon stick and nutmeg in the tagine base and cook over a low heat together until the apples begin to caramelize. Remove from the tagine and set to one side.

Wipe the tagine base, then add the oil to the tagine base. Heat over a medium heat, add the chicken thighs and cook until browned on all sides. Remove with a slotted spoon and set aside.

Add the onions and fry for 3–4 minutes until softened. Stir in the ground cinnamon, saffron, ginger and coriander leaves. Return the chicken to the tagine base, season with salt and pepper, pour in the measured water and stir well.

Bring to the boil, then reduce the heat to very low, cover with the lid and cook the chicken for 1½ hours until cooked through. Check occasionally that there is enough moisture in the tagine and, if necessary, add extra water as required.

Add the caramelized apples to the tagine and serve sprinkled with sesame seeds.

**Square Grill Pan
with Double Handles**

SERVES 6
Prep time: 15 minutes
Cooking time: 25 minutes

STUFFED HERB CHICKEN WITH CHERRY TOMATOES

Crispy griddled chicken with a delicious surprise inside

6 chicken thighs on the bone

85g mascarpone cheese

3 tablespoons olive oil

500g cherry tomatoes

For the herb sauce:

3 tablespoons olive oil

2 garlic cloves, finely chopped

4 canned anchovy fillets, drained
and finely chopped

2 tablespoons capers, drained
and finely chopped

1 tablespoon wholegrain mustard

1 handful of tarragon,
leaves chopped

1 handful of basil,
leaves chopped

1 handful of flat-leaf parsley,
leaves chopped

2 tablespoons lemon juice

Salt and freshly ground
black pepper

Mix together all the ingredients for the herb sauce and season with salt and pepper.

Using a sharp knife, make a cut in the thickest part of each chicken thigh to make a pocket.

Mix 60g of the herb sauce with the mascarpone and spoon 1 tablespoon of the mixture into each pocket. Close the opening and secure with a cocktail stick.

Brush the chicken with the oil and season with salt and pepper. Heat the grill pan over a high heat and grease with a little oil. Place half of the chicken in the pan and griddle for 5 minutes at a high temperature. Reduce the temperature and cook for another 10 minutes, covered. Carefully move the chicken thighs with a spatula so that they brown evenly. Turn the chicken over and griddle the other side for 10 minutes until golden brown and cooked through. Remove from the grill pan and keep warm, covered in a low oven, while you cook the remaining chicken.

Add the cherry tomatoes to the grill pan 5 minutes before the end of the cooking time and cook until softened.

Serve the chicken with the cherry tomatoes and any remaining herb sauce.

27cm Tagine

CHICKEN WITH OLIVES & PRESERVED LEMON

A classic tagine of slow-cooked chicken with olives, preserved lemons and spices.

SERVES 4
Prep time: 20 minutes
Cooking time: 1 hour 30 minutes

1 tablespoon olive oil

1kg whole chicken, cut into 8 pieces

2 onions, finely chopped

2 garlic cloves, chopped

2 tablespoons lemon juice

1 bunch of coriander, leaves chopped

1 teaspoon ground ginger

1 teaspoon ground cumin

A pinch of saffron threads

1 small cinnamon stick

200ml water or light chicken stock, plus extra as required

2 small preserved lemons, seeds removed and the skin cut into fine strips

120g black or green olives, pitted

Salt and freshly ground black pepper

Heat the oil in the tagine base over a medium heat, add the chicken pieces and cook until browned on all sides. Remove with a slotted spoon and set aside.

Add the onions and garlic and fry for 5–6 minutes until soft. Return the chicken to the tagine.

Stir in the lemon juice, half the coriander leaves, ginger, cumin, saffron, cinnamon stick and the measured water or stock. Reduce the heat to very low, cover with the lid and cook the chicken for 1½ hours until cooked through. Check occasionally that there is enough moisture in the tagine and, if necessary, add extra water or stock as required.

Rinse the preserved lemons and olives under cold running water to remove any excess salt and stir them into the tagine. Replace the lid and cook for a further 10 minutes.

Season the tagine with salt and pepper and sprinkle with the remaining coriander before serving.

NOTE: *Ask your butcher to portion the chicken for you.*

22cm Round Casserole

SERVES 4
Prep time: 25 minutes
Cooking time: 50 minutes

BELGIAN CHICKEN PIE WITH LIME & TARRAGON PESTO

A puff pastry crust is the perfect finishing touch for this creamy pie.

For the lime and tarragon pesto:

50g tarragon leaves

2 garlic cloves, peeled and left whole

25g toasted pine nuts

50g pecorino cheese, grated

Juice of 1 lime

150ml olive oil

Salt and freshly ground black pepper

For the stock:

1kg whole chicken

2 litres water

2 leeks, green part left whole, white part thinly sliced

3 celery sticks, 1 left whole, 2 sticks cut into small pieces

1 onion

3 thyme sprigs

1 bay leaf

For the pie:

20g butter

45g plain flour, plus extra for rolling

4–6 large waxy potatoes, peeled and cut into 2.5cm dice, par-boiled for 8 minutes

2 carrots, thinly sliced

½ fennel bulb, thinly sliced

300ml double cream

A pinch of cayenne pepper

250g ready-made puff pastry

1 egg, lightly beaten

For the pesto, put the tarragon, garlic, pine nuts, pecorino and lime juice in a blender and process until finely chopped. While blending, slowly drizzle in enough of the oil to make a smooth paste and season with salt and pepper.

For the stock, place the chicken in the casserole, add the measured water, the green part of the leeks, 1 whole celery stick, the onion, thyme and bay leaf. Season well with salt and pepper. Bring to the boil, then reduce the heat to medium, cover with the lid and simmer for 30 minutes.

Turn off the heat and let the chicken cool down in the stock. When cooled, lift the chicken from the stock, remove the skin and remove the cooked chicken from the carcass in large pieces. Strain the stock through a sieve and reserve.

Melt the butter in the casserole over a medium-low heat, add the flour and cook for 2 minutes, stirring. Stir in half of the strained stock and bring to the boil, stirring, until thickened. Continue to add the stock until the consistency of a thick cream soup.

Preheat the oven to 220°C. Stir the carrots, fennel, white part of the leeks, chopped celery, par-boiled potatoes and cream into the sauce. Return the cooked chicken pieces and season with cayenne pepper.

Lightly dust a work surface with flour and roll out the pastry into a circle large enough to cover the top of the casserole with a little overhang. Place the pastry over the top of the casserole, press the edges down and trim any excess. Brush the pastry top with the beaten egg and bake for 10–15 minutes until the pastry is golden and well risen.

Serve the chicken pie with the pesto.

27cm Tagine

SERVES 4
Prep time: 10 minutes
Cooking time: 1 hour 50 minutes

CHICKEN WITH ROOT VEGETABLES

The root vegetables add colour and flavour to this simple chicken tagine.

1 tablespoon olive oil

2 shallots, chopped

1 garlic clove, chopped

700g chicken thighs on the bone

1 teaspoon mild paprika

1 bay leaf

1 oregano sprig

1 rosemary sprig

2 tablespoons lemon juice

200ml water, plus extra as required

500g mixed root vegetables,
such as Jerusalem artichokes,
purple carrots, swede, baby turnips,
parsnips, cut into equal-sized pieces

Salt and freshly ground
black pepper

½ bunch of flat-leaf parsley,
leaves chopped, to garnish

Heat the oil in the tagine base over a medium heat, add the shallots and garlic and fry for 4–5 minutes until lightly caramelized.

Add the chicken thighs and sauté for 10 minutes, turning occasionally, until browned on all sides.

Stir in the paprika, bay leaf, oregano, rosemary, lemon juice and the measured water. Season with salt and pepper. Reduce the heat to very low, cover with the lid and cook the chicken for 1 hour.

After 1 hour, spread the root vegetables over the chicken in the tagine and mix everything well. Replace the lid and cook for a further 50 minutes, or until the vegetables are tender. Check occasionally that there is enough moisture in the tagine and, if necessary, add extra water or stock as required.

Sprinkle the parsley over before serving.

Cast Iron Rectangular Grill

SERVES 6
Prep time: 20 minutes
Cooking time: 15 minutes

HERB-CRUSTED TURKEY BROCHETTES

The herb, Parmesan and pine nut coating gives the turkey skewers a flavour boost and a crisp golden crust.

6 skinless, boneless turkey fillets, about 150g each

For the herb crust:

10 sage leaves

4 thyme sprigs, leaves only

4 flat-leaf parsley sprigs, leaves only

1 tablespoon dried basil

80ml olive oil, plus extra for brushing

3 tablespoons lemon juice

60g pine nuts

8 tablespoons breadcrumbs

40g Parmesan cheese, grated

For the herb crust, blend together the fresh and dried herbs with the oil, lemon juice and pine nuts to form a green sauce. Spoon the sauce into a bowl and stir in the breadcrumbs and Parmesan.

Add the turkey to the green sauce and turn until coated. Thread the turkey onto skewers. (If you are using wooden skewers, soak them for an hour in water before use to prevent them from charring or burning.)

Heat the grill pan over a medium-high heat and brush with oil. Griddle the turkey brochettes for 10–15 minutes, or until browned and cooked through, turning once. (Take care when turning them over.)

Why not serve the brochettes with baked potatoes, salad and a spoonful of soured cream?

27cm or 29cm Oval Casserole

TURKEY & APRICOTS IN ALE

Ale, rosemary and apricots add plenty of flavour to this rich turkey stew.

Serves 6
Prep time: 15 minutes
Cooking time: 1 hour 10 minutes

1kg skinless, boneless turkey thigh fillets, cut into 2.5cm cubes

2 tablespoons butter

2 tablespoons vegetable oil

450g fresh apricots, pitted and cut in half (or 8–9 dried apricots, cut in half, soaked in 250ml water for 1 hour and drained)

500ml light ale or Belgian beer, such as Gueuze

1 red onion, thinly sliced

2 garlic cloves, crushed

3 rosemary sprigs

100ml chicken stock

Salt and freshly ground black pepper

Season the turkey with salt and pepper.

Heat the butter and oil in the casserole over a medium heat, add half of the turkey and cook until browned on all sides. Remove with a slotted spoon and repeat with the remaining turkey, then set to one side.

Finely chop 4 of the apricots and add to the casserole with the browned turkey, light ale or beer, onion, garlic, 1 rosemary sprig and the stock. Bring to a simmer, reduce the heat to low and cook for 1 hour, stirring occasionally.

Pour the cooking sauce into a jug, retaining the casserole contents, and remove the rosemary sprig and any loose needles. Strain the cooking sauce to remove any lumps and pour it back into the casserole along with the casserole contents.

Add the remaining rosemary to the casserole with the rest of the apricots. Adjust the seasoning, to taste, then heat through until the apricots are tender and serve.

30cm Cast Iron Rectangular Dish

GUINEA FOWL
WITH PEARS & CIDER

A dish that captures the rich, traditional taste of Normandy.

SERVES 4
Prep time: 15 minutes
Cooking time: 50 minutes

2 guinea fowl, cut into pieces

20g butter

50ml Calvados

4 shallots, finely chopped

3 bay leaves

500ml cider

100ml chicken stock

6 pears, left whole and peeled

1 vanilla pod, split lengthways

20ml double cream

2 tablespoons cornflour

Salt and freshly ground black pepper

Season the guinea fowl with salt and pepper.

Preheat the oven to 175°C.

Heat the butter in the ovenproof dish over a medium heat, add the guinea fowl and cook until browned on all sides. Pour in the Calvados and cook until reduced.

Add the shallots and bay leaves and pour in the cider and chicken stock.

Arrange the pears in the dish and add the vanilla pod.

Cover with foil and roast the guinea fowl in the oven for 20 minutes. Remove the foil, add the cream and return the dish to the oven for another 15 minutes until the guinea fowl is cooked. If the sauce needs thickening, stir in the cornflour and cook for another 5 minutes. Remove the vanilla pod before serving.

24cm Round Casserole

HERB-STUFFED PIGEON WITH GRAPES

The gaminess of the pigeon works perfectly with the bacon and grapes in this casserole.

SERVES 6

Prep time: 20 minutes
Cooking time: 1 hour 10 minutes

6 oven-ready wood pigeons

1 bunch of flat-leaf parsley, chopped

1 bunch of tarragon, chopped

12 thin bacon rashers

50g butter

1 tablespoon olive oil

1 sweet white onion, chopped

2 garlic cloves, crushed

3 celery sticks, finely diced

1 tablespoon plain flour

300ml Muscat wine

560ml chicken stock

2 tablespoons wholegrain mustard

500g seedless black and white grapes

Salt and freshly ground black pepper

Preheat the oven to 170°C.

Season the pigeons with salt and pepper. Stuff the pigeons with the parsley and half of the tarragon. Wrap 2 bacon rashers around each pigeon.

Heat 1 tablespoon of the butter and the olive oil in the casserole over a medium heat, add three of the pigeons and cook until browned on all sides. Remove them from the casserole and repeat with the remaining pigeons, adding more oil, if necessary.

Add the onion, garlic and celery to the casserole and fry until soft. Add the remaining butter and when melted stir in the flour. Pour in the wine, stir and cook gently until reduced by half.

Return the pigeons to the casserole and add the stock and wholegrain mustard. Cover with the lid and transfer the dish to the oven to cook for 40 minutes.

Add the grapes and the remaining tarragon, cover and return the casserole to the oven for a further 10 minutes. Season with salt and pepper before serving.

27cm Tagine

BRAISED QUAILS WITH MEDJOOL DATES

Quails in an aromatic sauce with sticky dates and finished with toasted sesame seeds.

SERVES 4

Prep time: 15 minutes
Cooking time: 1 hour 10 minutes

2 tablespoons olive oil

4 oven-ready quails

2 small onions, finely chopped

150ml water or light chicken stock

1 small cinnamon stick

A pinch of saffron threads

⅓ teaspoon ground ginger

225g Medjool dates, pitted and cut in half

10g butter

2 teaspoons honey

Salt and freshly ground black pepper

2 tablespoons sesame seeds (optional), to garnish

Heat 1 tablespoon of the oil in the tagine base over a medium heat, add two of the quails and cook until browned on all sides. Remove the quails and set to one side while you cook the two remaining quails, adding more oil if necessary. Set all the quails to one side.

Add the remaining oil and fry the onions, stirring occasionally, until lightly caramelized.

Add the measured water or stock to the tagine base with the cinnamon stick, saffron and ginger and season with salt and pepper. Bring the sauce to the boil and return the quails to the tagine.

Reduce the heat to very low, cover with the lid and cook for 40 minutes.

Stir the dates, butter and honey into the tagine. Replace the lid and cook for a further 15 minutes until the quails are cooked. Adjust the seasoning to taste with salt and pepper, and serve sprinkled with sesame seeds, if liked.

DUCK LEGS WITH BEETROOT & CARAWAY

A rich and comforting combination of duck and root vegetables.

27cm Tagine

SERVES 2
Prep time: 20 minutes
Cooking time: 2 hours 45 minutes

2 duck legs

2 small onions, finely chopped

1 garlic clove, chopped

1 bouquet garni

½ teaspoon caraway seeds

100ml red wine

½ chicken stock cube

350g uncooked beetroots,
cut into quarters and thickly sliced

2 carrots, thickly sliced

Salt and freshly ground black pepper

1 bunch of flat-leaf parsley,
leaves chopped, to garnish

Using the tip of a sharp knife, make diagonal cuts into the skin of each duck leg.

Put the duck legs, skin-side down, in the tagine base and cook over a low heat for 10 minutes until the fat starts to run and the skin is golden.

Add the onions and garlic to the duck, increase the heat to medium and fry for 5 minutes until soft.

Pour off any excess oil then add the bouquet garni, caraway seeds and red wine and crumble in the stock cube. Season with salt and pepper. Reduce the heat to low, cover with the lid and cook the duck legs for 2 hours, or until tender. Check occasionally that there is enough moisture in the tagine and, if necessary, add some water as required.

Add the beetroots and carrots to the tagine. Replace the lid and cook for a further 30 minutes over a low heat, or until the vegetables are tender. Sprinkle with parsley before serving.

20cm Square Ceramic Dish

SERVES 4
Prep time: 20 minutes
Cooking time: 1 hour 15 minutes

DUCK WITH GLAZED TURNIPS
Duck and ale are an unusual combination but they work together beautifully in this dish.

25g butter

4 duck breasts

4 rosemary sprigs, needles removed in small sprigs

8 small turnips, cut into quarters

12 small waxy potatoes, cut into small even-sized pieces

1 tablespoon brown sugar

1 bottle dark ale, about 330ml

100ml chicken stock

1 teaspoon cornflour

Salt and freshly ground black pepper

Preheat the oven to 175°C.

Put the butter in the ovenproof dish and heat it in the oven until melted.

Using the tip of a sharp knife, make diagonal cuts into the skin of each duck leg. Insert the rosemary sprigs in the gaps between the skin and the meat and season with salt and pepper.

Arrange the duck breasts in the butter-coated dish, cover with foil, and cook in the oven for 45 minutes.

Remove the dish from the oven and pour off any excess fat. Add the turnips and potatoes, sprinkle over the sugar and season with salt and pepper.

Turn the oven down to 160°C. Pour the ale and stock into the dish, stir and return it to the oven for 30 minutes, or until the vegetables are tender.

Remove the dish from the oven and thicken the sauce with the cornflour, if needed. Adjust the seasoning, to taste, and serve in the dish.

Round Grill Pan

DUCK, PRUNE & ORANGE BROCHETTES

A modern twist on the French classic duck à l'orange.

SERVES 6
Prep time: 20 minutes, plus marinating
Cooking time: 10 minutes

---

12 dried prunes, pitted and cut in half

2 tablespoons Armagnac

4 rosemary sprigs, needles finely chopped

2 tablespoons pink peppercorns

½ teaspoon fine sea salt

3 duck breast fillets, about 200g each, fat removed and cut into 2.5cm cubes

1 large orange, cut into bite-sized pieces

A few bay leaves

Juice of ½ orange

Olive oil, for brushing

Soak the prunes in the Armagnac for 30 minutes until softened, then drain, discarding the Armagnac.

Crush the rosemary needles with the pink peppercorns and salt in a pestle and mortar. Rub the duck in half of the rosemary mixture.

Thread the duck onto skewers, interspersed with pieces of orange, bay leaves and prune. Repeat to make 6 skewers in total. (If you are using wooden skewers, soak them for an hour in water before use to prevent them from charring or burning.)

Squeeze a little orange juice over the skewers, brush with oil and sprinkle over the rest of the rosemary mixture.

Heat the grill pan over a high heat and lightly brush with oil. Put the brochettes in the grill pan and griddle, turning them occasionally so they do not burn, until the duck is cooked and starting to colour.

Square Grill Pan

RABBIT BROCHETTES WITH SAGE & LEMON

Perfect for lunch on a hot summer's day.

SERVES 6

Prep time: 15 minutes, plus marinating
Cooking time: 15 minutes

750g rabbit fillets

3 courgettes, sliced into ribbons

Oil, for brushing

For the marinade:

Peel and juice of 1 lemon

2 garlic cloves

2 sage sprigs, leaves removed

100ml olive oil

Salt and freshly ground pepper

For the marinade, blanch the lemon peel in boiling water for 2 minutes, then rinse immediately in cold water. Finely chop the lemon peel, garlic and sage leaves. Add the olive oil and season with salt and pepper.

Place the rabbit pieces in one bowl and the courgette ribbons in another. Divide the marinade between the bowls, stir, and leave to marinate for 2 hours.

Thread the rabbit fillets onto skewers. (If you are using wooden skewers, soak them for an hour in water before use to prevent them from charring or burning.) Set to one side.

Heat the grill pan over a high heat and lightly brush with oil. Griddle the courgette ribbons for 5 minutes, or until blackened in places. Remove and set to one side.

Cook the duck brochettes for 5–6 minutes on each side. Serve the rabbit brochettes with the courgettes and add a squeeze of lemon juice before serving.

22cm or 24cm Round Casserole

SERVES 4
Prep time: 20 minutes
Cooking time: 1 hour 15 minutes

RABBIT IN GORGONZOLA SAUCE

A surprising and delicious combination of rabbit and pears in a creamy cheese sauce.

1 prepared rabbit, cut into pieces

25g butter

1 tablespoon olive oil

2 garlic cloves, sliced

1 sage sprig, leaves sliced,
plus extra to garnish

100ml white port

500ml chicken stock

400ml double cream

200g Gorgonzola cheese, crumbled

2 pears, peeled, cored
and cut into wedges

Salt and freshly ground black pepper

Season the rabbit with salt and pepper.

Melt the butter and oil in the casserole over a medium heat, add the rabbit and cook for 10 minutes until browned on all sides. Stir in the garlic and sage.

Pour in the port and cook, stirring to remove any brown bits stuck to the bottom of the casserole, until reduced. Add the chicken stock and bring to the boil. Cover with the lid, reduce the heat to low and simmer for 1 hour, turning the rabbit occasionally.

Remove the rabbit from the casserole with a slotted spoon and keep it warm. Bring the sauce in the casserole to the boil, stir in the cream and cook until reduced and thickened.

Stir the Gorgonzola into the sauce and season with salt and pepper.

Add the pears and return the warm rabbit pieces to the casserole. Heat through to piping hot and serve garnished with the extra sage.

NOTE: *Ask your butcher to prepare the rabbit for you.*

FISH & SEAFOOD

SOUTH AFRICAN SEAFOOD STEW (POTJIEKOS)

An authentic fish and shellfish stew that packs a powerful punch.

22cm or 24cm Casserole

SERVES 4
Prep time: 20 minutes, plus marinating
Cooking time: 35 minutes

For the piri piri marinade:

Juice of 2 lemons

2 tablespoons vegetable oil

1 tablespoon chopped coriander

2–4 fresh chillies, deseeded and chopped

2 garlic cloves, peeled

For the seafood stew:

500g firm white fish fillets, such as bream, bass, monkfish or gurnard, skinned and cut into pieces

1 tablespoon butter

2 red onions, cut into quarters

3 potatoes, cut into wedges

2 tomatoes, cut into quarters

400ml fish stock, plus extra if required

1 teaspoon ground ginger

8 dried apricots

100g large raw prawns, heads removed and deveined

100g cooked mussels in their shell

A few coriander sprigs, to garnish

For the piri piri marinade, put the lemon juice, 1 tablespoon of the oil, coriander leaves, chillies and garlic in a mini food processor and pulse to a paste.

Put the white fish in a non-metallic dish, spoon over the marinade and turn until combined. Cover and leave the fish to marinate in the refrigerator for at least 30 minutes.

Heat the remaining oil and the butter in the casserole over a medium heat, add the onions and potatoes and fry for 5 minutes, or until the onions are soft.

Add the tomatoes, fish stock, ginger and apricots, bring to a simmer and cook for 15 minutes.

Add the marinated fish to the sauce. Check that there is enough sauce and add extra stock, if needed. Simmer the fish for 10 minutes, then add the prawns and cook for a further 5 minutes until pink. A couple of minutes before the prawns are cooked, stir in the mussels and heat through. Garnish with coriander sprigs before serving.

Cast Iron Rectangular Grill

GRILLED FISH WITH TOMATOES & OLIVES

Light and summery, this simple fish dish captures the flavours of the Mediterranean.

SERVES 6
Prep time: 15 minutes
Cooking time: 10 minutes

6 whole fish, such as trout or whiting, gutted and cleaned

1 teaspoon dried oregano

1 teaspoon dried thyme

3 lemons, cut in half and sliced

6 tablespoons lemon oil

500g cherry tomatoes, cut in half

80g green olives

A few flat-leaf parsley sprigs, leaves chopped

Salt and freshly ground black pepper

Heat the grill pan over a high heat.

Score the skin of each fish on both sides. Season with the oregano, thyme, salt and pepper and fill the cavity of the fish with some of the lemon slices.

Brush the hot grill with some of the lemon oil. Arrange the fish in the grill pan and scatter over the remaining lemon slices. Griddle the fish for 3–4 minutes on each side until the skin is crisp and golden and the fish just cooked through. Turn the fish carefully so you do not damage the skin.

Mix the tomatoes with the olives and parsley. Pour over a little of the lemon oil and season with salt and pepper. Serve the fish, spooning over any juices in the pan, with the tomato, olives and parsley, and some crusty bread.

27cm Tagine

SERVES 4
Prep time: 15 minutes
Cooking time: 50 minutes

PISTACHIO-CRUSTED COD WITH TOMATOES & CAPERS
Fish fillets topped with a nutty crust and cooked with a cherry tomato and caper sauce.

4 tablespoons olive oil

5 shallots, finely chopped

2 garlic cloves, finely chopped

A pinch of mild paprika

2 tablespoons salted capers, rinsed and drained

2 bay leaves

700g cherry tomatoes

500g cod fillet, skinned, boned and cut into 4 pieces

Salt and freshly ground black pepper

For the pistachio crust:

2 tablespoons shelled unsalted pistachios, chopped

½ bunch of flat-leaf parsley, leaves chopped

½ bunch of coriander, leaves chopped

5 chives, snipped

Heat 2 tablespoons of the oil in the tagine base over a medium heat, add the shallots and garlic and fry for 1 minute. Mix in the paprika and fry for a further 4–5 minutes, stirring occasionally, until the shallots are soft.

Add the capers, bay leaves and tomatoes. Season with a pinch of salt and stir everything together. Reduce the heat to low, cover with the lid and cook for 30 minutes. Check occasionally to see if there is enough moisture in the tagine and, if needed, add some water as required.

For the pistachio crust, mix the pistachios, parsley, coriander and chives in a bowl with the remaining 2 tablespoons of oil and season with salt and pepper.

Spread the pistachio crust over the pieces of fish and place them in the tagine on top of the tomato mixture. Replace the lid and cook for 10–15 minutes, depending on the thickness of the fish. Serve straightaway.

COD & POTATO CASSEROLE
A light and healthy fish casserole with a hint of orange.

24cm Round Casserole

SERVES 4
Prep time: 10 minutes
Cooking time: 45 minutes

3 tablespoons olive oil

1 red onion, sliced

300g potatoes, scrubbed and sliced

1 leek, sliced

50ml dry white wine

150ml fish stock

1½ courgettes, sliced

400g cod steaks, boned
and cut into 2 pieces

2–3 dill sprigs

100ml milk

2 spring onions, chopped

Zest and juice of ½ orange

Salt and freshly ground black pepper

Heat the oil in the casserole over a medium heat, add the onion and potatoes and fry for 5 minutes until the onion is soft. Add the leek and mix well.

Pour in the wine, bring to the boil and cook until it is reduced by half. Add the stock, cover with the lid and reduce the heat to low. Cook gently for 20 minutes until the potatoes are almost tender.

Add the courgettes, cod and dill to the casserole. Cover with the lid and cook for a further 15 minutes until the cod is cooked and flakes apart easily.

Stir in the milk, season with salt and pepper and heat through.

Stir in the spring onions and the orange zest and juice and serve.

27cm Tagine

SERVES 3
Prep time: 15 minutes
Cooking time: 1 hour

CITRUS, CHILLI & CORIANDER-MARINATED SWORDFISH

Swordfish steaks in a feisty citrus marinade cooked with spiced new potatoes.

300g new potatoes,
peeled and sliced

½ teaspoon ground cumin

½ teaspoon ground coriander

3 bay leaves

150ml water, plus extra as required

3 swordfish steaks

½ lemon, cut in half

Salt and freshly ground black pepper

For the marinade:

3 garlic cloves, chopped

1 bunch of coriander, leaves chopped

1 small red chilli, deseeded and cut into fine strips

Juice of 2 lemons

2 tablespoons olive oil

Place the potato slices in the tagine base, stir in the cumin, coriander and bay leaves, pour over the measured water and season with salt and pepper. Cover with the lid and cook the potatoes over a low heat for 40 minutes, or until almost tender. Check occasionally to see if there is enough moisture in the tagine and, if needed, add extra water as required.

Meanwhile make the marinade: mix together the garlic, coriander leaves, chilli, lemon juice and oil in a large, shallow dish. Place the swordfish steaks in a non-metallic dish and spoon the over marinade. Cover and marinate in the refrigerator for 30 minutes.

Remove the dish from the fridge, take the fish out of the marinade and place it on top of the potatoes. Pour the marinade over, replace the lid and cook for a further 15–20 minutes, or until the fish is just cooked and the potatoes are tender. Squeeze over extra lemon juice, to taste, just before serving.

Square Grill Pan

SWORDFISH, CHORIZO & SUN-DRIED TOMATO BROCHETTES

The fish is flavoured with smoky chorizo, basil and rich sun-dried tomatoes – perfect for a light summery meal.

SERVES 6
Prep time: 30 minutes, plus marinating
Cooking time: 10 minutes

600g swordfish or monkfish, membrane removed, cut into 2.5cm cubes

12 thick slices of chorizo

12 basil leaves

12 sun-dried tomatoes in oil, drained

1 teaspoon paprika

Salt and freshly ground black pepper

For the marinade:

8 tablespoons olive oil

3 tablespoons balsamic vinegar

1 tablespoon port

Thread a piece of fish, a slice of chorizo, a basil leaf and a sun-dried tomato on a brochette stick, then repeat so each skewer has two of each. Make 6 skewers in total, then season with pepper and the paprika. (If you are using wooden skewers, soak them for an hour in water before use to prevent them from charring or burning.)

Mix together all the ingredients for the marinade in a non-metallic shallow dish. Season with salt and pepper. Spoon the marinade over the brochettes in the dish and leave to marinate for at least 15 minutes, or until ready to cook.

Heat the grill pan over a high heat. Add the brochettes, spoon over some of the marinade and cook for 5 minutes on each side, or until the fish is cooked.

Serve the brochettes with a crisp salad.

MONKFISH WITH OLIVES & CHARLOTTE POTATOES

Meaty fish in a spicy sauce with green olives, new potatoes and preserved lemon.

27cm Tagine

SERVES 4
Prep time: 20 minutes
Cooking time: 1 hour 10 minutes

1 tablespoon olive oil

1 garlic clove, chopped

1 small red pepper, deseeded and sliced

125ml dry white wine

1 bunch of coriander, tied together with kitchen string

1 teaspoon ground cumin

1 teaspoon mild paprika

1 teaspoon hot paprika

½ teaspoon ground turmeric

300g Charlotte new potatoes, cut in half lengthways

150ml water, plus extra as required

1 preserved lemon, rinsed, pulp and pips discarded, skin cut into small dice

150g green olives, rinsed and pitted

650g skinned, boned monkfish, membrane removed, cut into 8 pieces

Salt and freshly ground black pepper

Heat the oil in the tagine base over a low heat, add the garlic and red pepper and fry for 10 minutes, stirring regularly, until soft. Increase the heat to medium, pour in the white wine and cook for 5 minutes until reduced.

Add the bunch of coriander, cumin, mild and hot paprika, turmeric, potatoes, the measured water and a little salt.

Reduce the heat to low, cover with the lid and cook for 40 minutes, or until the potatoes are nearly cooked. Check occasionally to see if there is enough moisture in the tagine and, if needed, add some extra water as required.

Add the preserved lemon, olives and the monkfish pieces to the tagine and gently combine. Replace the lid and cook for a further 15 minutes, or until the fish is just cooked. Remove the coriander bunch and season to taste before serving.

27cm or 29cm Oval Casserole

SEA BREAM WITH CITRUS

Fish cooked in a delicious combination of citrus fruits and fresh herbs.

SERVES 4

Prep time: 20 minutes
Cooking time: 15 minutes

2 sea bream, about 350g each, gutted and cleaned

4 limes, peeled

8 dill sprigs

6 mint sprigs

6 tarragon sprigs

2 pink pomelos or 1 pink grapefruit, peeled

2 oranges, peeled

2 lemons, peeled

1 tablespoon olive oil

1 tablespoon butter

2 garlic cloves, sliced

2 shallots, sliced

1 red chilli, deseeded and finely chopped

4 bay leaves

400ml fish stock

Salt and freshly ground black pepper

Season the fish inside and out with salt and pepper. Cut three of the limes into thin wedges. Stuff the bream with the sprigs of dill, mint and tarragon and the lime wedges.

Cut the pomelos or grapefruit, oranges, lemons and the remaining lime into segments, cutting between the white membranes with a small sharp knife. Do this over a bowl to catch any juices and reserve.

Heat the oil and butter in the casserole over a medium heat, add the garlic, shallots, chilli and bay leaves and fry for 1–2 minutes until softened. Add the stuffed fish, the citrus fruit and any reserved juices and cook for 3 minutes.

Pour the stock over the fish, cover with the lid and cook over a low heat for 5–10 minutes, or until the fish is cooked through. The cooking time will depend on the thickness of the fish.

The bream is delicious served with new potatoes.

32cm Rectangular Ceramic Dish

BAKED SEA BASS IN SALT CRUST
The salt crust keeps the fish moist and flavoursome while it bakes.

SERVES 4
Prep time: 15 minutes
Cooking time: 30 minutes

2 sea bass

2 rosemary sprigs

2 thyme sprigs

2 sage sprigs

1 lime, peeled and cut into thin wedges, plus extra to serve

1kg coarse sea salt

2 egg whites

For the tomato and almond sauce:

1 shallot, peeled

1 tomato

1 egg

1 teaspoon mustard

20ml red wine vinegar

50ml olive oil

25g ground almonds

Salt and freshly ground black pepper

Preheat the oven to 180°C.

Season the sea bass with pepper. Stuff the fish with the herb sprigs and lime wedges.

Mix the sea salt and egg whites into a paste. Spoon a thin layer of the paste in the ovenproof dish. Lay the sea bass on top and cover completely with the remaining paste. Bake for 30 minutes.

Meanwhile, make the tomato and almond sauce. Put the shallot, tomato, egg, mustard and vinegar in a blender. Blend until combined, then gradually pour in the oil. Add the ground almonds, season with salt and pepper and blend until smooth and creamy.

To serve, break open the salt crust surrounding the sea bass. Fillet the fish using a spoon and fork and arrange on serving plates. Serve with the tomato and almond sauce on the side and extra wedges of lime.

27cm Tagine

SERVES 4
Prep time: 15 minutes
Cooking time: 1 hour 5 minutes

SEA BASS WITH CHERRY TOMATOES, LEMON & POTATOES

A light, summery white fish tagine in a lemon sauce with cherry tomatoes and new potatoes.

1kg small new potatoes, scrubbed or peeled and cut in half

1 garlic clove, chopped

1 bunch of coriander, leaves chopped

Juice of 2 lemons

4 bay leaves

½ teaspoon ground coriander

¼ teaspoon hot chilli powder

3 tablespoons olive oil

300g yellow and red cherry tomatoes, cut in half if large

100ml water, plus extra as required

600g skinned and boned sea bass, cut into 4 pieces

Salt and freshly ground black pepper

1 teaspoon fennel seeds, to garnish

Place the potatoes, garlic, coriander leaves, lemon juice, bay leaves, ground coriander, chilli powder, 2 tablespoons of the oil and the cherry tomatoes in the tagine. Season with salt and pepper and pour over the measured water.

Cover with the lid and cook over a very low heat for 50 minutes. Check occasionally that the vegetables are not sticking to the bottom of the tagine and add extra water as required.

Lay the sea bass on top of the vegetables, season with a little salt and pepper and drizzle over the remaining oil. Cover and continue to cook for 10–15 minutes until the fish is just cooked. The cooking time will depend on the thickness of the fish.

Sprinkle with the fennel seeds before serving.

NOTE: *This recipe also works well with monkfish or halibut.*

Square Grill Pan

SALMON FILLETS WITH ASIAN SALAD

The Asian dressing in this recipe is a combination of salty, sweet and sour – delicious with the bean sprout salad and salmon fillets.

SERVES 6
Prep time: 10 minutes
Cooking time: 10 minutes

80g bean sprouts

2 tablespoons toasted sesame seeds

Coconut oil, for cooking

6 salmon fillets, about 200g each

A few dill sprigs, to garnish

For the dressing:

Finely grated zest and juice of 2 limes

2 tablespoons plum sauce

2 tablespoons rice vinegar

1 tablespoon sesame oil

1 tablespoon light soy sauce

Salt and freshly ground black pepper

For the dressing, mix together all the ingredients and season with a little salt and pepper.

Mix the bean sprouts with 1 tablespoon of the sesame seeds and spoon over a few tablespoons of the dressing. Set to one side.

Heat the grill pan over a high heat. Lightly oil the pan with the coconut oil and griddle the salmon, skin-side down first, for 2–3 minutes until the skin is crisp. Turn the salmon over and cook the other side until almost cooked through, but still slightly pink in the middle.

Remove the salmon from the pan and leave to rest for a few minutes. Season the fish with salt and pepper and garnish with a few sprigs of dill.

Serve with the bean sprout salad and extra dressing on the side.

BAKED HADDOCK WITH LEMON BUTTER SAUCE

Haddock cooked simply in a lemony butter sauce – what could be better?

20cm Oval Cast Iron Dish

SERVES 4
Prep time: 10 minutes
Cooking time: 15 minutes

4 thick haddock fillets

50g butter

4 shallots, thinly sliced

2 lemons, cut in half

¼ bunch of flat-leaf parsley, leaves chopped

Salt and freshly ground black pepper

Preheat the oven to 180°C.

Score the skin of each haddock or cod fillet with a sharp knife, to prevent it curling during cooking. Season the fillets with salt and pepper.

Heat the butter in the ovenproof dish in the oven until melted and starting to brown.

Arrange the fish in the dish, spoon over the melted butter, and cook in the oven for 5 minutes.

Scatter over the shallots, spoon over any juices in the bottom of the dish and return it to the oven for another 5–10 minutes until the haddock is just cooked and the shallots have softened. The cooking time will depend on the thickness of the fillets.

Remove from the oven, season with more pepper, squeeze over the juice from one of the lemons and scatter with the parsley.

Cut the remaining lemon into four wedges to serve with the fish.

Delicious with slices of buttered brown bread.

NOTE: *This recipe also works well with cod.*

27cm Tagine

SERVES 4
Prep time: 10 minutes
Cooking time: 1 hour 5 minutes

HADDOCK WITH FENNEL IN A CREAM SAUCE

Poached haddock with potatoes and fennel, cooked in fish stock with cream.

500g waxy new potatoes, scrubbed and cut into large dice

1 fennel bulb, sliced

Lovage or celery leaves from 2 sticks, chopped

2 bay leaves

150ml fish stock

150ml double cream

400g skinned and boned haddock, cut into large pieces

Salt and freshly ground black pepper

A few flat-leaf parsley sprigs, leaves roughly chopped, to garnish

Place the potatoes, fennel, lovage or celery leaves and bay leaves in the tagine base. Pour the fish stock and cream over the vegetables and season with salt and pepper. Mix the ingredients together and cover with the lid. Cook over a very low heat for 50 minutes, or until the potatoes are tender. Check occasionally to see if there is enough moisture in the tagine and, if needed, add some water as required.

Lay the pieces of haddock on top of the potatoes, cover and cook for a further 15 minutes over a very low heat, or until the fish is cooked. Sprinkle the chopped parsley over the fish just before serving.

Rectangular Grill Pan

GRILLED STUFFED MACKEREL WITH FRESH HERBS & CHEESE

Fragrant fresh herbs and creamy soft cheese make a light filling for fresh mackerel.

SERVES 6
Prep time: 15 minutes
Cooking time: 15 minutes

1 small egg, lightly beaten

300g cream cheese

A few mint sprigs, finely chopped

A few flat-leaf parsley sprigs, finely chopped, plus extra to garnish

A few dill sprigs, finely chopped

A few chervil sprigs, finely chopped

12 mackerel, gutted and cleaned

3 tablespoons olive oil

1 lemon, cut in half

Salt and freshly ground black pepper

Mix half of the beaten egg into the cream cheese. If the cheese is still firm, add more of the egg, but the mixture should not be too runny. Mix in the herbs and season with salt and pepper.

Stuff the mackerel, or fish of choice, with the cheese mixture and secure with kitchen string. Brush the mackerel with oil and season with pepper.

Heat the grill pan over a high heat, add the mackerel and griddle for 5 minutes on each side. (You may need to cook the fish in batches.) Griddle the lemon at the same time, cut-side down.

Carefully cover the pan with foil and cook for a further 5 minutes over a low heat until the filling is warmed through.

Place the mackerel on a serving plate and squeeze over the juice from the lemons.

Serve with any leftover herb cheese sauce and a spinach and walnut salad, if liked.

NOTE: *This recipe also works well with herring, sardines or red mullet.*

32cm Rectangular Ceramic Dish

BACON-WRAPPED TROUT WITH FENNEL & ANISEED

The combination of fennel, aniseed and pastis add a distinctive flavour to the trout.

SERVES 2–4
Prep time: 15 minutes
Cooking time: 40 minutes

50g butter

2 fennel bulbs, bulbs thinly sliced, fronds reserved

20ml pastis

20ml water

2 large trout, gutted and cleaned

4 bacon rashers

A few thyme sprigs

Salt and freshly ground black pepper

Chopped dill, to garnish (optional)

Preheat the oven to 160°C.

Melt the butter in the ovenproof dish.

Arrange the fennel slices in the dish with the melted butter and season with salt and pepper.

Pour the pastis and the measured water over the fennel and place in the oven for 15 minutes until softened.

Meanwhile, season the trout all over with pepper and wrap each one in two bacon rashers.

Increase the oven temperature to 175°C. Place the trout on top of the braised fennel with the thyme and cook for a further 25 minutes until the fish is cooked.

Sprinkle with the reserved fennel fronds, or if you don't have any fronds finish with some chopped dill.

Rectangular Grill Pan

COURGETTE & ANCHOVY BRUSCHETTA
Perfect as a summer appetizer.

SERVES 6
Prep time: 5 minutes
Cooking time: 20 minutes

6 slices of ciabatta

Olive oil, for brushing

1½ tablespoons chilli oil

Juice of 1 small lemon

1 courgette, sliced lengthways

6 anchovy fillets

1 teaspoon oregano leaves

Salt

Preheat the grill pan over a high heat.

Brush the ciabatta slices with the olive oil and griddle on each side until golden brown.

Mix together the chilli oil and three-quarters of the lemon juice, then brush the mixture over the courgette slices and season with salt. Arrange the courgette in the grill pan and griddle until blackened in places and tender. Remove and set aside.

Rub the anchovies with olive oil and griddle for 5 minutes, turning once, or until cooked.

Top the ciabatta with the courgette slices and anchovies. Squeeze over the rest of the lemon juice and sprinkle with oregano.

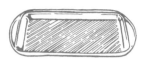

GRILLED SQUID WITH FENNEL & POMEGRANATE DRESSING

Packed with flavour, this warm squid salad features fresh lime, chilli, herbs and pomegranate.

XL Rectangular Grill

SERVES 6
Prep time: 20 minutes
Cooking time: 15 minutes

800g whole squid, gutted and cleaned

2 fennel bulbs, bulbs sliced, fronds reserved

Olive oil, for brushing

Finely grated zest of 1 lime

1 red chilli, deseeded and finely chopped

1 handful of mint leaves, leaves chopped

1 handful of flat-leaf parsley, leaves chopped

2 red onions, sliced into rings

For the pomegranate dressing:

1 pomegranate, cut in half

8 tablespoons olive oil

1 tablespoon honey

4 limes, cut in half

Salt and freshly ground black pepper

For the dressing, slice the pomegranate in half and remove the seeds by hitting the peel side of the pomegranate with some force with a wooden spoon. Collect any juices at the same time.

Mix together the oil, 3 tablespoons of the pomegranate juice and the honey until combined. Add 3 tablespoons of the pomegranate seeds.

Heat the grill pan over a medium heat.

Place the limes, cut-side down, in the grill pan and griddle for 5 minutes. Remove and squeeze the juice from three of the limes into the dressing. Season with salt and pepper, taste and add extra honey, if needed. Set the remaining lime to one side.

Slice open the squid and cut in half. Using the tip of a sharp knife, lightly score a diamond pattern over each squid half and season with a little salt and pepper.

Brush the fennel with some of the oil and season with salt and pepper. Place the fennel in the grill pan and griddle for 5 minutes, turning once, until golden. Spoon the fennel onto a serving plate and scatter over the lime zest, chilli and herbs.

Brush the squid with oil and arrange in the grill pan and griddle for 1–2 minutes on each side, depending on its thickness – do not overcook the squid as it can become tough. Remove from the heat, add the fennel, red onions and fennel fronds to the squid. Drizzle the dressing over the top and serve immediately with the remaining lime.

30cm Shallow Casserole

SERVES 4
Prep time: 20 minutes
Cooking time: 35 minutes

COCONUT CLAM CURRY

**Coconut lends a creaminess and tames
the heat of the Venus clam curry.**

2 tablespoons groundnut oil

6 cardamom pods, split

6 bay leaves

2 teaspoons mustard seeds

2 small cinnamon sticks

1 large onion, finely chopped

4 garlic cloves, crushed

2 green chillies, deseeded and
finely diced

2 tablespoons ground cumin

2 tablespoons ground coriander

2 teaspoons ground turmeric

1kg pumpkin or squash, peeled,
deseeded and cut into 2.5cm dice

100ml water

375ml coconut milk

600g Venus clams, prepared, any
clams with broken shells discarded

Salt

A few coriander sprigs, to garnish

Heat the oil in the casserole over a medium heat, add the cardamom, bay leaves, mustard seeds and cinnamon sticks and fry for 1–2 minutes until the flavours are released.

Add the onion and garlic and continue to fry for 2–3 minutes. Stir in the chillies, cumin, coriander and turmeric and cook for another 1 minute or until the onion is soft. Add the pumpkin or squash and cook for 5 minutes, stirring often.

Pour in the measured water and coconut milk. Bring to the boil, then turn the heat down and simmer for 15 minutes, or until the sauce is reduced and the pumpkin or squash is tender. The flavour can be adjusted by adding extra coconut milk, ground cumin and coriander, depending on your taste.

Stir the clams into the sauce, cover with the lid and simmer until the clam shells open. Discard any unopened shells and season the sauce with salt.

Garnish with the coriander sprigs and serve with boiled rice, if liked.

CRAB WITH CORIANDER, CHILLI & LIME

Delicious brown crab cooked in a fresh lime and coriander butter sauce with a hint of chilli.

27cm Tagine

SERVES 4
Prep time: 20 minutes
Cooking time: 25 minutes

2 cooked brown female crabs, about 800g each

1 tablespoon olive oil

3 garlic cloves, chopped

200ml dry white wine

2cm fresh root ginger, peeled and grated

2 bunches of coriander, leaves chopped

½ teaspoon coriander seeds, ground

3 spring onions, sliced diagonally, plus extra to garnish

1 red Thai chilli, deseeded and cut into fine strips

Juice of 2 limes

100g softened butter

1 tablespoon flour

Salt

To prepare the crabs, twist off the claws and legs, remove and discard the stomach sac and grey gills from the carapace (shell body) and retain the crabmeat. Cut the crab body into large pieces.

Heat the oil in the tagine base over a medium heat, add the garlic and fry for 1 minute. Add the wine, bring to the boil then turn the heat to low and cook until reduced.

Add the ginger, fresh and ground coriander, spring onions, chilli, lime juice, crab legs, claws and the crab shells to the tagine.

Combine the softened butter with the flour then stir it into in the tagine, reduce the heat to very low, cover with the lid and cook the crab for 20 minutes.

Season with salt and garnish with extra spring onions. Serve with plenty of napkins!

24cm or 26cm Round Casserole

SERVES 4
Prep time: 20 minutes
Cooking time: 35 minutes

CRAB-STUFFED BEEFSTEAK TOMATOES

Brimming with flavour, these ripe beefsteak tomatoes are filled with a herby crab mixture.

5 beefsteak tomatoes

1 shallot, finely chopped

2 garlic cloves, finely chopped

2–3 thyme sprigs, leaves chopped

3 oregano sprigs, leaves chopped

2–3 rosemary sprigs, needles chopped

400g prepared crabmeat

1 slice of wholemeal bread, crusts removed, processed into crumbs

5 tablespoons couscous

175ml vegetable stock

Salt and freshly ground black pepper

Preheat the oven to 200°C.

To prepare the tomatoes, cut off the top of each one and remove the pulp and seeds carefully with a spoon. Finely chop the pulp with the seeds and set to one side.

To make the filling, mix together the shallot, garlic, herbs, crabmeat, breadcrumbs, uncooked couscous and the finely chopped tomato pulp. Season with salt and pepper.

Fill the tomatoes with the crab mixture, replace the tomato tops and put them into the casserole. Pour over the vegetable stock, cover with the lid and bake in the oven for 30–35 minutes until the couscous is tender.

31cm x 26cm Rectangular Ceramic Dish

SERVES 4
Prep time: 15 minutes
Cooking time: 20 minutes

LOBSTER WITH MOROCCAN SPICES

Treat yourselves to lobster in an aromatic spiced butter.

2 cooked lobsters, about 650g each

100g butter

2 teaspoons ras el hanout

200g rocket leaves

1 teaspoon olive oil

2 lemons, cut into wedges

Salt and freshly ground black pepper

Preheat the oven to 175°C.

Cut the lobsters in half and remove the stomach and the intestinal tract. Remove the rubber bands from the claws.

Melt the butter in the dish in the oven, remove and stir in the ras el hanout.

Place the lobsters in the dish, spoon over the spiced butter and bake for 20 minutes until heated through.

Mix the rocket with the oil and season with salt and pepper.

Arrange the lobsters on a warm serving plate and spoon over the cooking juices. Top with the rocket salad and serve with the wedges of lemon.

A crusty baguette goes well with the lobster.

27cm Tagine

SERVES 4
Prep time: 15 minutes
Cooking time: 20 minutes

PRAWNS WITH CHERMOULA

Large prawns infused with a garlic, herb and chilli-spice marinade and cooked in a tagine.

500g large shell-on prawns, heads removed and deveined

For the chermoula:

2 garlic cloves, crushed

1 small bunch of flat-leaf parsley, leaves chopped

1 bunch of coriander, leaves chopped

1 tablespoon mild paprika

1 teaspoon ground ginger

1 teaspoon ground cumin

Juice of 1 lemon

2 tablespoons olive oil

¼ teaspoon coarse sea salt

¼ –½ teaspoon cayenne pepper or harissa paste, to taste

2–3 tablespoon water

For the chermoula, mix together all the ingredients in a medium-sized bowl, adding the cayenne or harissa paste to taste. Mix in enough of the measured water to make a thick sauce.

Stir in the prepared prawns, turning to coat them in the chermoula, then transfer everything to the tagine base and cover with the lid.

Place the tagine over a low heat and cook the prawns for 15–20 minutes, depending on their size, until cooked.

NOTE: *Harissa pastes can vary greatly in flavour and heat, so start with the smaller quantity first.*

18cm Round Cast Iron Dish

SERVES 4
Prep time: 15 minutes
Cooking time: 20 minutes

SCAMPI WITH MUSHROOMS & COURGETTE

A simply delicious dish of baked shrimp and vegetables – perfect for a light meal with crusty bread.

16–24 scampi (large prawns), depending on size, heads removed, peeled, tails left on, deveined

2 tablespoons olive oil

1 garlic clove, chopped

2 shallots, chopped

150g shiitake mushrooms, sliced

150g oyster mushrooms, sliced

150g chestnut mushrooms, sliced

150g button mushrooms, sliced or left whole if small

1 courgette, scooped into balls using a melon baller

Salt and freshly ground black pepper

1 tablespoon each of chopped chervil, dill, parsley, tarragon and oregano, to garnish

Preheat the oven to 180°C.

Season the scampi with salt and pepper and coat in 1 tablespoon of the oil.

Heat the remaining oil in the ovenproof dish over a medium heat on the hob, add the garlic, shallots, mushrooms and courgette balls and fry for 5–8 minutes, or until soft. Season with salt and pepper.

Scatter the scampi over the top of the vegetables and place the dish in the oven for 10 minutes, or until the scampi is cooked.

Meanwhile, mix together all the herbs. Remove the scampi from the oven and scatter the herbs over before serving.

**Square Plancha
with Double Handles**

SERVES 6

*Prep time: 25 minutes, plus marinating
Cooking time: 10 minutes*

MARINATED PRAWNS WITH FRESH HERB SAUCE

Packed with flavour, the prawns are marinated in a chilli, spice and lime marinade and served with a herb yogurt sauce.

1.2kg prawns, unpeeled or peeled, depending on preference, deveined

2 kaffir lime leaves (optional)

2 limes, cut into wedges

For the spice marinade:

1 red chilli, deseeded and finely chopped

1 green chilli, deseeded and finely chopped

3 garlic cloves, chopped

½ teaspoon salt

1 handful of coriander, leaves chopped

2 teaspoons ground cumin

2 teaspoons ground coriander

1 teaspoon paprika

3 tablespoons lime juice

4 tablespoons olive oil, plus extra for brushing

For the fresh mint sauce:

A few mint sprigs, leaves finely chopped

A few coriander sprigs, leaves finely chopped

1 red onion, finely chopped

100ml plain yogurt

1 teaspoon fish sauce

1 teaspoon lime juice

Freshly ground black pepper

For the spice marinade, grind the chillies, garlic and salt in a pestle and mortar. Stir in the spices, lime juice and enough of the olive oil to make a rough paste.

Place the prawns in a large, non-metallic dish, spoon the marinade over and turn until combined. Cover and leave to marinate in the refrigerator for 3 hours, turning occasionally.

Meanwhile, for the mint sauce, mix together all the ingredients in a bowl. Season with pepper and keep the sauce, covered, in the fridge until ready to use.

Heat the grill pan over a medium heat and brush with oil. Add the lime leaves, if using. Using a slotted spoon, remove the prawns from the marinade and place them in the pan. Griddle the prawns for 5–8 minutes, turning once, until cooked.

Serve the prawns with the mint sauce and wedges of lime – a baked potato and salad are good accompaniments, too.

VEGETABLE DISHES

30cm Shallow Casserole

RISOTTO WITH A TRIO OF CHEESES
A tasty vegetarian risotto with a peppery rocket finish.

SERVES 4
Prep time: 15 minutes
Cooking time: 25 minutes

1 tablespoon olive oil

3 tablespoons butter

2 shallots, finely chopped

1 celery stick, finely chopped

275g arborio risotto rice

5 tablespoons dry sherry

1 litre hot vegetable stock

150g frozen peas

50g Parmesan cheese,
finely grated

30g blue cheese of choice

250g small mozzarella balls

1 handful of rocket leaves

Freshly ground black pepper

Heat the oil and 2 tablespoons of the butter in the casserole over a medium heat, add the shallots and celery and fry for 2–3 minutes until softened. Stir in the rice and when all the grains are translucent, add the sherry and cook, stirring, until absorbed.

Add 100ml of the hot stock and stir constantly, paying special attention to the bottom and the sides of the pan, until absorbed by the rice. Now, add the stock a few spoonfuls at a time while continuing to stir. Wait for the stock to be absorbed before adding the next few spoonfuls. Make sure the rice is kept at simmering point and, if needed, adjust the heat.

After 15 minutes, add the peas and continue stirring while adding the stock. After 20 minutes, test if the rice is 'al dente', or almost cooked, and the risotto is a thick, soupy consistency. At this point, stir in the Parmesan, blue cheese and the remaining butter and remove the pan from the heat.

Season with pepper and just before serving, stir in the mozzarella balls and top with the rocket leaves.

20cm Square Ceramic Dish

SERVES 4
Prep time: 15 minutes
Cooking time: 40 minutes

RICE WITH MEDITERRANEAN VEGETABLES

Delicious as a side dish to a meat, fish or vegetarian meal.

½ courgette, cut into 5mm cubes

½ aubergine, cut into 5mm cubes

½ fennel bulb, cut into 5mm cubes

½ red pepper, deseeded and cut into 5mm cubes

½ green pepper, deseeded and cut into 5mm cubes

1 red onion, finely chopped

2 plum tomatoes, chopped

2 garlic cloves, finely chopped

2 tablespoons olive oil

1 tablespoon herbes de Provence

150g long-grain rice

1 litre chicken stock

Salt and freshly ground black pepper

Basil leaves, to garnish

Preheat the oven to 160°C.

Mix all the vegetables with the oil, herbes de Provence and rice, season with salt and pepper and spoon the mixture into the ovenproof dish. Roast for 10 minutes, or until the vegetables are starting to soften.

Remove the dish from the oven, then pour over the stock and stir well.

Return the dish to the oven, cover with foil and cook for a further 30 minutes, stirring frequently, until the rice is cooked. Garnish with basil before serving.

SPRING VEGETABLE CASSEROLE

Broad beans, asparagus... Spring is in the air!

24cm Round Casserole

SERVES 4
Prep time: 10 minutes
Cooking time: 15 minutes

1 tablespoon olive oil

2 garlic cloves, crushed

4cm piece fresh root ginger, grated

100ml sherry

125g bulgar wheat

14 asparagus spears,
woody ends discarded

500g broad beans, shelled

5 spring onions, finely chopped

200g frozen peas

2 bay leaves

600ml vegetable or chicken stock

Salt and freshly ground black pepper

1 small handful of parsley and mint,
leaves chopped, to garnish

Heat the oil in a casserole over a medium heat, add the garlic and ginger and fry for 1 minute. Pour in the sherry and cook until reduced.

Add the bulgar wheat, asparagus, broad beans, spring onions, peas and bay leaves and fry for 4 minutes, stirring. Add the stock, stir and cover with the lid. Simmer for 10–12 minutes until the vegetables are tender and the bulgar is cooked.

Season with salt and pepper and garnish with the parsley and mint just before serving.

22cm Round Casserole

CHICKPEA & SPINACH CASSEROLE

A quick, lightly spiced vegetarian casserole, full of healthy ingredients.

SERVES 4
Prep time: 10 minutes
Cooking time: 15 minutes

1 tablespoon vegetable oil

1 red onion, chopped

2 garlic cloves, crushed

1 small green chilli, deseeded and chopped

2 teaspoons ground ginger

¼–½ teaspoon sea salt

2 x 400g cans chickpeas, drained

1 teaspoon ground cumin

½ teaspoon ground turmeric

6 tablespoons water

250g cherry tomatoes, cut in half

150g baby spinach leaves

1 tablespoon lemon juice

Salt and freshly ground black pepper

Heat the oil in the casserole over a medium heat, add the onion, garlic, chilli, ginger and sea salt and fry for 5 minutes until the onion is soft.

Stir in the chickpeas, cumin and turmeric and season with pepper. Pour in the measured water and stir until it has been absorbed.

Add the cherry tomatoes and cook for a further 3 minutes. Remove from the heat and stir in the spinach and lemon juice until the leaves are wilted. Taste and season with extra salt and pepper, if needed.

SPICED ROASTED PEPPER SOUP

The roasted peppers give this soup a smoky sweetness and vibrant colour.

22cm or 24cm Round Casserole

SERVES 4
Prep time: 15 minutes
Cooking time: 40 minutes

6 large ripe tomatoes

1 tablespoon olive oil

1 red onion, finely chopped

1 red chilli, deseeded and finely chopped

1 jar of roasted red peppers, about 350g drained weight, drained, rinsed and chopped

4 thyme sprigs

1 bay leaf

1 tablespoon curry powder

600ml vegetable stock

A splash of double cream (optional)

Salt and freshly ground black pepper

To skin the tomatoes, put them in a bowl and pour over boiling water to cover. Leave for 1–2 minutes, then drain, cut a cross at the stem end of each tomato and peel off the skins. Remove and discard the seeds, roughly chop the tomato pulp, then set to one side.

Heat the oil in the casserole over a medium heat, add the onion and chilli and fry for 2–3 minutes until softened. Add the roasted peppers and chopped tomatoes, 3 thyme sprigs, bay leaf and curry powder and cook for a further 5 minutes.

Pour in the stock, cover with the lid and cook for 30 minutes over a low heat.

Remove the bay leaf and thyme sprigs. Transfer the soup to a blender or processor and blend until smooth.

Return the soup to the casserole, heat through and season with salt and pepper. Serve topped with cream, if liked, and the remaining sprig of thyme.

NOTE: *Instead of using a jar of roasted peppers, you could roast your own. For this soup, brush 6 peppers with olive oil (and reduce the quantity of tomatoes to three). Place on a hot grill pan and griddle, turning occasionally, until the skins begin to blister and blacken. Place the roasted peppers in a bowl, cover with cling-film and leave to cool. Peel off the skins, retaining any juices, then remove the seeds and cut the peppers into slices. You could also roast the peppers in the oven or under a grill.*

4 x Ceramic Petite Casseroles

EGGS EN COCOTTE WITH ASPARAGUS

A simply delicious breakfast, light meal or snack.

SERVES 4
Prep time: 5 minutes
Cooking time: 15 minutes

2 teaspoons melted butter

8 small asparagus spears,
woody ends discarded, cut in half

4 large eggs

Salt and freshly ground black pepper

Crusty bread and watercress sprigs,
to serve

Preheat the oven to 200°C.

Grease the individual casseroles with the melted butter and add some salt and pepper.

Place the asparagus pieces into the base of the casseroles and break an egg into each one. Season again with salt and pepper.

Lay a sheet of baking paper in a deep oven dish, large enough to hold the casseroles. Place the casseroles into the dish and pour in enough hot water to come two-thirds of the way up the sides. Place the dish in the oven and cook for 15 minutes, or until the eggs are cooked to your liking.

Serve with crusty bread and watercress on the side.

27cm Tagine

SERVES 4
Prep time: 15 minutes
Cooking time: 55 minutes

SWEET PEPPERS WITH EGGS
A tasty dish, perfect for a weekend brunch.

4 tomatoes

2 tablespoons olive oil

1 large red onion, finely chopped

2 garlic cloves, chopped

6 mixed peppers (red, yellow and orange), deseeded, stalks removed, and sliced

1 small red or green chilli, deseeded and finely chopped

1 teaspoon fennel seeds

100ml water

4 eggs

Salt and freshly ground black pepper

To skin the tomatoes, put them in a bowl and pour over boiling water to cover. Leave for 1–2 minutes, then drain, cut a cross at the stem end of each tomato, and peel off the skins. Remove the seeds, dice the tomatoes and set to one side.

Heat the oil in the tagine base over a medium heat, add the onion and garlic and fry for 5 minutes until the onion is soft.

Add the sliced peppers, chilli and fennel seeds. Season with salt and pepper. Stir in the diced tomatoes and the measured water. Reduce the heat to low, cover with the lid and cook for 45 minutes, stirring occasionally.

Five minutes before the end of the cooking time, make 4 spaces in the vegetables with the back of a spoon. Break in the eggs, replace the lid and continue to cook until the eggs are set. Serve the tagine immediately.

NOTE: *You could try using a mixture of mini peppers and quail's eggs.*

27cm Tagine

SERVES 4
Prep time: 10 minutes
Cooking time: 1 hour 30 minutes

SLOW-COOKED TOMATOES WITH HONEY & CINNAMON

Serve these sweet-spiced tomatoes warm or cold with cold cuts or cheeses.

1kg tomatoes, a mixture of different varieties, colours and sizes

4 tablespoons olive oil

2 cinnamon sticks, cut in half lengthways

3 bay leaves

½ teaspoon ground turmeric

1 tablespoon roughly chopped thyme

2 tablespoons honey

Salt and freshly ground black pepper

Prepare the tomatoes by cutting some of them in half and removing the seeds of the larger ones with a teaspoon.

Pour 2 tablespoons of the oil into the tagine base and add the tomatoes. Arrange the cinnamon sticks and the bay leaves between the tomatoes.

In a small bowl, mix together the turmeric, thyme, honey and the remaining 2 tablespoons of oil. Spoon the mixture over the tomatoes, season with salt and pepper and cover with the lid.

Place the tagine over a very low heat and cook the tomatoes for 1½ hours, or until tender. Check occasionally that the tomatoes are not sticking to the bottom and, if needed, add a little water. Serve warm or cold in the tagine.

Reversible Grill Pan

SERVES 6
Prep time: 10 minutes
Cooking time: 25 minutes

OREGANO & RICOTTA-STUFFED TOMATOES

Serve as a side dish with barbecued food, or as a main with new potatoes.

6 large firm tomatoes, cut in half

1 tablespoon olive oil

200g ricotta cheese

60g spinach, finely chopped

1 teaspoon dried oregano

Freshly grated nutmeg, to taste

2 tablespoons pine nuts

2 slices of bread, crusts removed and processed into crumbs

50g Parmesan cheese, finely grated

Salt and freshly ground black pepper

Brush the cut half of each tomato with the oil and season with salt and pepper.

Mix together the ricotta, spinach, oregano and nutmeg in a bowl and season with salt and pepper.

Heat the grill pan over a medium heat and toast the pine nuts until starting to colour. Remove the nuts from the pan and set to one side.

Grill the breadcrumbs in the same pan until toasted then remove, set aside and wipe the pan clean.

Return the grill pan to the heat and griddle the halved tomatoes, cut-side down, until slightly blackened. Turn them over and top with a good spoonful of the ricotta mixture. Sprinkle with the Parmesan.

Cover with a lid or foil, making sure the they do not touch the tomatoes. Turn the heat to low and cook the tomatoes for 8–10 minutes until warmed through but they still hold their shape.

Sprinkle the breadcrumbs and pine nuts over the top of the tomatoes before serving.

You could serve the tomatoes with a spinach salad.

AUBERGINES STUFFED WITH RICE, HERBS & PINE NUTS

Healthy, light and nutritious – perfect as a starter or light meal.

27cm Tagine

SERVES 4
Prep time: 15 minutes, plus salting
Cooking time: 55 minutes

2 small aubergines,
cut in half lengthways

Coarse sea salt, for salting

3 tablespoons olive oil

½ onion, finely chopped

1 garlic clove, chopped

½ bunch of chives, leaves chopped

½ bunch of dill, leaves chopped

½ bunch of flat-leaf parsley,
leaves chopped

40g toasted pine nuts

1 teaspoon dried mint

70g cooked white rice

½ teaspoon mild paprika

175ml water, plus extra as required

Juice of 1 small lemon

Salt and freshly ground black pepper

Dill sprigs, to garnish

To prepare the aubergines, carefully scoop out the pulp with a spoon and set the halves to one side. Coarsely chop the pulp and place it in a strainer. Sprinkle with coarse sea salt and leave the aubergine pulp to stand for 30 minutes.

Rinse the aubergine pulp thoroughly under cold running water, then drain and pat it dry with kitchen paper.

Heat 2 tablespoons of the oil in the tagine base over a medium-low heat and fry the onion and garlic until soft. Add the aubergine pulp and fry for 8–10 minutes until starting to turn golden.

Spoon the cooked aubergine mixture into a bowl and stir in the herbs, pine nuts, dried mint, cooked rice and paprika. Season with salt and pepper.

Spoon the herb mixture into the aubergine halves. Place them in the tagine base with the filling upwards and pour in the measured water, the remaining oil and the lemon juice.

Cover with the lid and set the tagine over a low heat for 40 minutes until the stuffed aubergines are cooked through. Check occasionally that the aubergines are not sticking to the bottom and, if needed, add a little extra water.

Garnish with sprigs of dill and serve with pitta bread, if you like.

Rectangular Grill Pan

AUBERGINE, PESTO & MOZZARELLA STACKS

Slices of pesto-coated aubergine are filled with mozzarella and fresh basil then cooked in a grill pan until golden – delicious!

SERVES 6
Prep time: 15 minutes, plus salting
Cooking time: 10 minutes

4 aubergines, cut into 24 x 1cm thick slices, ends discarded

250g buffalo mozzarella, drained and cut into 12 slices

12 large basil leaves, plus extra to garnish

12 cherry tomatoes, cut in half

For the pesto:

40g Parmesan cheese, finely grated

2 handfuls of basil

1 garlic clove

150ml olive oil

40g pine nuts

Juice of 1 lemon

Salt and freshly ground black pepper

Sprinkle the aubergines with salt and leave for 30 minutes, then rinse under cold running water and pat dry.

Meanwhile, make the pesto: put all the ingredients, excluding the lemon juice, in a blender and blend until finely chopped. Add the lemon juice and season with salt and pepper.

Brush one side of each aubergine slice with pesto.

Place 12 of the aubergine slices, pesto-side down, on a work surface and top each one with a slice of mozzarella, a basil leaf and two halves of cherry tomato. Season with pepper. Place a second slice of aubergine on top, pesto-side up, to make a 'sandwich' and press firmly together.

Heat the grill pan over a high heat, add the aubergine stacks and griddle for 5 minutes on each side until tender and golden. Serve immediately, garnished with extra basil.

30cm Shallow Casserole

SERVES 4
Prep time: 15 minutes
Cooking time: 20 minutes

AUBERGINE SALSA
**An aubergine salsa with plenty of zing –
serve as a side dish or as a meal with couscous or rice.**

---

2 tablespoons olive oil,
plus extra if required

3 large aubergines,
cut into 4–5cm long slices

4 oregano sprigs

2 red onions, cut into wedges

2 garlic cloves, crushed

2 tablespoons capers in vinegar,
drained

4 tablespoons white wine vinegar

1 tablespoon balsamic vinegar

2 tablespoons extra-virgin olive oil

2 tablespoons shelled unsalted
pistachios, chopped

50g Parmesan cheese,
sliced into shavings

Salt and freshly ground black pepper

Heat the oil in the casserole over a medium heat, add the aubergines and oregano and fry, stirring, for 3–4 minutes until browned on all sides.

Add the onions and garlic to the casserole and fry for a further 3–4 minutes, adding a little extra oil if the casserole is too dry.

Stir in the capers and wine vinegar, cover with the lid and cook over a low heat for 10 minutes, or until the vegetables are tender. Season with salt and pepper.

Pour the balsamic vinegar and extra-virgin olive oil over the salsa and scatter with the pistachios and Parmesan shavings.

Couscous or rice make good accompaniments.

18cm or 20cm Round Casserole

SERVES 4
Prep time: 15 minutes, plus cooling
Cooking time: 50 minutes

PEA SOUFFLÉ
A warm and comforting soufflé made in a casserole dish.

500g fresh peas, shelled

25g butter, plus extra for greasing

3 tablespoons plain flour

200ml milk

Freshly grated nutmeg, to taste

2 large eggs, separated

40g Parmesan cheese, finely grated

2 tablespoons chopped basil leaves

50g breadcrumbs

50g pine nuts

Salt and freshly ground
black pepper

Preheat the oven to 180°C.

Cook the peas in the casserole in lightly salted water until tender. Drain and rinse them immediately under cold running water to keep their bright green colour. Purée the cooked peas in a blender until smooth and season with salt and pepper. Set to one side.

To make a béchamel sauce, melt the butter in the casserole over a low heat. Add the flour and cook for 1 minute, stirring. Add the milk, a little at a time, while stirring continuously, until you have a smooth, creamy sauce. Grate in the nutmeg, to taste, and season with salt and pepper. Pour the sauce into a jug and leave to cool.

Combine the egg yolks with the pea purée, Parmesan and basil and stir the mixture into the cooled béchamel sauce until combined. Whisk the egg whites in a clean bowl until they form stiff peaks then fold them into the egg yolk and pea mixture.

Wash and dry the casserole then grease the inside with the extra butter and dust with the breadcrumbs.

Pour the soufflé mixture into the casserole. Sprinkle the pine nuts over the top and cook for 40 minutes, or until puffed up and golden. To check if it is ready, prick with a skewer and if it comes out dry, the soufflé is cooked.

Serve immediately.

27cm or 29cm Oval Casserole

ITALIAN BRAISED VEGETABLES

Braised vegetables that capture the authentic flavours of the Mediterranean.

SERVES 6
Prep time: 20 minutes
Cooking time: 40 minutes

6 baby artichokes

Juice of 1 lemon

50ml olive oil

2 lemons, cut into wedges

2 garlic cloves, finely chopped

3–4 lemon thyme sprigs

2 bay leaves

1 fennel bulb, cut into 8 pieces, green fronds reserved and chopped

350g baby new potatoes, scrubbed and cut in half

50ml Pernod Ricard

100–125ml vegetable stock

A pinch of saffron threads

Salt and freshly ground black pepper

Cut the stems from the artichokes, remove the tough outer leaves, trim the tips, then cut them in half. Add the lemon juice to some water in a bowl and plunge the artichokes into the liquid to prevent them discolouring. Set to one side.

Heat the oil in the casserole over a medium heat, add the lemon wedges, garlic, lemon thyme and bay leaves and cook, stirring for 2–3 minutes. Stir in the fennel and potatoes.

Drain the artichokes, add them to the casserole and cook for a few more minutes. Pour in the Pernod Ricard and cook until reduced, then add the stock and saffron and bring the contents to the boil.

Reduce the heat, cover with the lid and simmer for 30–35 minutes until the potatoes are tender, adding extra stock, if necessary. Season to taste with salt and pepper, and serve garnished with the reserved fennel fronds.

24cm x 19cm Rectangular Ceramic Dish

SERVES 4
Prep time: 20 minutes
Cooking time: 45 minutes

PROVENÇAL ROASTED VEGETABLES

Typical of Provence, this medley of roasted vegetables can be served warm or cold as a salad.

2 garlic cloves,
peeled and cut in half

3 tablespoons olive oil

1 tablespoon herbes de Provence

1 red chilli, deseeded
and thinly sliced

2 red onions, cut into wedges

2 red peppers, deseeded
and cut into wedges

2 green peppers, deseeded
and cut into wedges

1 aubergine, cut into quarters,
and each quarter into wedges

1 courgette, thickly sliced

½ fennel bulb, cut into wedges

2 plum tomatoes, cut in half

2 large mushrooms, cut into quarters

1 teaspoon coarse sea salt

Preheat the oven to 160°C.

Mix the garlic with the oil, herbs and chilli.

Put the onions, red and green peppers, aubergine, courgette, fennel, tomatoes and mushrooms in the ovenproof dish, pour the flavoured oil over and turn until combined. Season with the coarse sea salt.

Roast in the oven for 45 minutes, turning occasionally, until the vegetables are cooked. Serve warm or cold as a salad.

27cm Tagine

ASPARAGUS WITH SAFFRON CREAM

Asparagus in a saffron-scented creamy sauce.

SERVES 4
Prep time: 10 minutes
Cooking time: 25 minutes

1 tablespoon olive oil

24 white or green asparagus spears, woody ends discarded, stems peeled

A generous pinch of saffron threads

100ml vegetable stock

100ml single cream

Salt and freshly ground black pepper

Heat the oil in the tagine base over a medium heat, add the asparagus and sauté on all sides until lightly coloured. Add the saffron, pour the vegetable stock over and season with salt and pepper.

Place the lid on the tagine, reduce the heat to low and cook the asparagus for 15–20 minutes, depending on their size, until tender.

Divide the asparagus between 4 preheated serving plates. Add the cream to the stock in the tagine and heat gently until warm but not hot.

Adjust the seasoning to taste, then pour the sauce over the asparagus. Serve immediately.

27cm Tagine

MOROCCAN-SPICED HERITAGE CARROTS

The Moroccan spice mixture, ras el hanout, complements the sweet taste of the striking heritage carrots.

SERVES 4
Prep time: 15 minutes
Cooking time: 50 minutes

3 tablespoons olive oil

650g heritage carrots (purple, yellow and white), cut in half lengthways, then cut into 4 diagonal pieces

2 garlic cloves, peeled and left whole

1 teaspoon ras el hanout

A pinch of chilli powder

30g currants

2 bay leaves

150ml water

Juice of 1 small lemon

½ bunch of flat-leaf parsley, leaves chopped

½ bunch of coriander, leaves chopped

30g toasted pine nuts

Salt

Heat 2 tablespoons of the oil in the tagine base over a low heat. Add the carrots, garlic, ras el hanout, chilli powder, currants, bay leaves and the measured water. Mix everything together, cover with the lid and cook the carrots for 50 minutes, or until tender.

Remove the garlic from the tagine and crush with the lemon juice and the remaining oil in a pestle and mortar until smooth.

Add the garlic and lemon paste to the cooked carrots and stir in the parsley, coriander and toasted pine nuts.

Season to taste with salt and serve.

27cm Tagine

SPICED SQUASH WITH RAISINS

A colourful and fragrant dish with a hint of Moroccan spice – perfect as a side to roasted meats and fish.

SERVES 4
Prep time: 15 minutes, plus soaking
Cooking time: 40 minutes

150ml warm water

2 teaspoons orange flower water

30g raisins

1 tablespoon olive oil

1 small onion, finely chopped

1 teaspoon ras el hanout

½ teaspoon ground cumin

150ml vegetable stock

800g butternut squash, cut in half, deseeded and cut into thick slices

1 cinnamon stick

30g blanched almonds, coarsely chopped

Salt and freshly ground black pepper

Pour the warm water into a bowl, stir in the orange flower water and the raisins and leave them to soak for 30 minutes.

Heat the oil in the tagine base over a medium heat, add the onion and fry until lightly caramelized.

Mix together the ras el hanout, cumin and vegetable stock. Season with salt and pepper and stir the mixture into the caramelized onion.

Place the squash slices in the tagine and add the cinnamon stick and the soaked, drained raisins. Cover with the lid, reduce the heat to low and cook the squash for 40 minutes, or until tender.

Sprinkle the almonds over the squash just before serving.

27cm Tagine

SERVES 4
Prep time: 10 minutes
Cooking time: 1 hour

BRAISED CHICORY WITH HONEY & ORANGE
Tender chicory finished with a butter, honey and orange glaze.

8 large chicory, cut into 2 or 3 pieces, depending on size, discarding the core

200ml vegetable stock

2 tablespoons honey

40g butter

½ teaspoon pared orange zest

1 tablespoon olive oil

Salt and freshly ground black pepper

Arrange the chicory in the tagine base and pour the vegetable stock over. Season with salt and pepper. Cover with the lid and cook the chicory for 50 minutes over a low heat.

Remove the lid and add the honey, butter, orange zest and oil. Increase the heat to medium and cook the chicory, without the lid, for a further 10 minutes, turning them occasionally until caramelized on all sides. Serve in the tagine.

CAULIFLOWER WITH GARLIC CHIPS

Simple braised whole cauliflower with fried slices of garlic.

27cm Tagine

SERVES 4
Prep time: 10 minutes
Cooking time: 1 hour

300ml water, plus extra as required

1 teaspoon ground turmeric

1 tablespoon olive oil,
plus extra for frying

1 cauliflower, outer leaves and
woody stem removed, blanched
for 10 minutes

7 garlic cloves, thinly sliced

Salt and freshly ground
black pepper

Heat enough oil to generously cover the base of the tagine. Add the garlic to the hot oil and fry quickly until golden brown. Remove the slices with a slotted spoon, drain on kitchen paper, season with salt and pepper and set aside. Wipe the base of the tagine clean.

Mix together the measured water, ground turmeric and 1 tablespoon of the oil in a bowl and season to taste with salt and pepper. Place the cauliflower in the tagine base, pour the turmeric mixture over and cover with the lid.

Place the tagine over a very low heat and cook the cauliflower for around 1 hour, or until tender. Check occasionally that the cauliflower is not dry and, if needed, add a little extra water.

Serve the cauliflower in the tagine with the fried garlic sprinkled over the top.

DESSERTS

POACHED PEARS IN WINE, HONEY & GINGER

Sweet pears poached in wine with honey, ginger and a hint of spice

27cm Tagine

SERVES 6
Prep time: 10 minutes
Cooking time: 1 hour 20 minutes

6 firm ripe dessert pears, Williams or Conference, peeled and stalks left on

2 tablespoons lemon juice

300ml sweet white wine

1cm piece fresh root ginger, peeled and thinly sliced

½ teaspoon ground black peppercorns

2 tablespoons soft brown sugar

2 tablespoons mild honey

30g butter

To prepare the pears, carefully remove the core from the base of each one and brush all over with the lemon juice to prevent them discolouring.

Place the cored pears upright in the tagine base and pour over the wine. Place on the hob over a medium heat and bring the wine to the boil.

Add the ginger, peppercorns, sugar, honey and butter. Cover with the lid, reduce the heat to low and poach the pears for 1 hour–1 hour 20 minutes, depending on their size and degree of ripeness. Occasionally baste the pears with the cooking juices while cooking.

Serve the pears in the tagine or in warmed bowls.

**Square Plancha
with Double Handles**

SERVES 6
Prep time: 10 minutes
Cooking time: 25 minutes

CARAMELIZED ORCHARD FRUIT WITH CALVADOS SAUCE

The Norman apple brandy, Calvados, adds the finishing touch to this dessert.

1 vanilla pod, sliced lengthways and seeds scraped out

3 tablespoons caster sugar

1 teaspoon ground cinnamon

40g melted butter

3 apples, cored and cut into quarters

3 pears, cored and cut into quarters

50ml Calvados

2 tablespoons roasted hazelnuts

Mix the vanilla seeds, sugar and cinnamon with the melted butter.

Brush the apples and pears with the spiced butter.

Heat the plancha over a medium heat, add the apples and pears and cook, turning occasionally, until caramelized. Remove the pan from the heat, pour in the Calvados then flambé the fruit. Leave to cool slightly.

Cover the pan with a lid or foil and cook for a further 8–10 minutes over a low heat. Serve the fruit, with any juices spooned over, and sprinkled with roasted hazelnuts.

The caramelized fruit is also delicious in a pancake with a scoop of ice cream.

27cm Tagine

FIVE-SPICE & VANILLA POACHED APPLES

Sweet spice and vanilla-infused apples – perfect with ice cream or thick plain yogurt.

SERVES 4
Prep time: 10 minutes
Cooking time: 1 hour 30 minutes

30g salted butter, diced

4 dessert apples, cored and sliced

1 vanilla pod, split lengthways
and seeds scraped out

70g caster sugar

⅓ teaspoon Chinese five-spice

150ml water, plus extra as required

Place the butter in the tagine base and arrange the apples on top.

Mix the vanilla seeds with the sugar and five-spice, then sprinkle the mixture over the apples. Pour the measured water over the apples and cover with the lid.

Place the tagine over a very low heat and poach the apples for 1½ hours. Check occasionally that there is enough moisture in the tagine and, if needed, add extra water as required.

Serve the apples warm or at room temperature with yogurt or ice cream.

**25cm Cast Iron Tatin Dish,
or Round Ceramic Pie Dish**

SERVES 4
Prep time: 15 minutes
Cooking time: 30 minutes

TARTE TATIN
Everyone's favourite classic apple pie!

60g butter

**4 apples, peeled, cut in half,
cored and cut into 1cm thick slices**

8 tablespoons caster sugar

1 sheet of ready-roll puff pastry

Preheat the oven to 220°C.

Spread the butter over the base of the tatin dish and melt it in the oven.

Arrange the apple slices in the dish. Sprinkle over the sugar, return the dish to the oven and bake until the apples are soft and caramelized.

Meanwhile, unroll the pastry and cut it into a 27cm round. Prick it all over with a fork and carefully place the pastry on top of the apples. Tuck the pastry over the apples down the inside of the dish and return to the oven for another 15 minutes, or until the pastry is cooked and golden.

Leave to cool slightly then turn out the tatin onto a large plate. Serve warm with cream or ice cream.

BLOOD ORANGES WITH CAMPARI & HONEY

A simple dessert of blood oranges with a hint of spice.

27cm Tagine

SERVES 4
Prep time: 15 minutes
Cooking time: 1 hour 30 minutes

400ml Campari

200ml water

3 tablespoons orange blossom honey

1 bay leaf

2 black peppercorns

4 blood oranges, peeled

Pour the Campari and the measured water into the tagine base. Add the honey, bay leaf and peppercorns and bring the contents to the boil over a medium heat.

Add the oranges to the tagine, reduce the heat to low, cover with the lid and poach the oranges for 1½ hours, or until tender.

Serve the oranges in dessert bowls with some of the poaching juice spooned over.

ALMOND PUDDING WITH PINK GRAPEFRUIT

Caramel-topped almond pudding with a citrus base.

27cm Tagine

SERVES 4
Prep time: 15 minutes
Cooking time: 35 minutes

Butter, for greasing

3 pink grapefruits,
peeled and segmented

2 eggs

100g caster sugar,
plus extra for dusting

150g ground almonds

200ml whipping cream

1 tablespoon orange flower water

½ vanilla pod, split lengthways
and seeds scraped out

Freshly ground black pepper

Preheat the oven to 180°C.

Grease the tagine base with butter and add the grapefruit segments, arranging them into a fan shape.

In a mixing bowl, beat the eggs with the sugar until light and fluffy. Fold in the ground almonds, whipping cream, orange flower water and vanilla seeds, then add a grinding of pepper on top.

Pour the sponge mixture over the grapefruit segments in the tagine. Cover with the lid and bake for 30 minutes.

Towards the end of the cooking time, preheat the grill to high, or turn the oven to grill. Remove the lid from the tagine and sprinkle a thin layer of sugar over the top of the sponge. Place the tagine base under the grill to caramelize the sugar; keep an eye on it to prevent it burning.

Serve the dessert warm in the tagine or leave to cool.

22cm x 17cm Rectangular Ceramic Dish

SERVES 4
Prep time: 10 minutes
Cooking time: 15 minutes

CARAMELIZED PINEAPPLE WITH KIRSCH

The cherry liqueur adds a kick to the caramelized sauce for the pineapple.

50g butter

50g caster sugar

50ml kirsch

1 pineapple, skin removed, cored and cut into chunks

100g mixed dried berries and raisins

100g flaked almonds

Mint sprigs, to decorate

Preheat the oven to 175°C.

Melt the butter in the ovenproof dish, then stir in the sugar. Return to the oven for 5 minutes until caramelized.

Add the kirsch to the dish and stir in the pineapple, mixed berries and raisins and the almonds.

Turn the oven to a medium-high grill, then grill the pineapple for 5 minutes until starting to colour.

Remove the dish from the oven and serve the pineapple with a scoop of coconut ice cream, decorated with mint sprigs.

Round Grill Pan

GRILLED PEACHES WITH AMARETTO & AMARETTI CRUMBLE
Two Italian indulgences in one irresistible dessert!

SERVES 6
Prep time: 10 minutes, plus marinating
Cooking time: 10 minutes

6 fresh peaches,
or the equivalent canned

100ml Amaretto

100g mascarpone

150g curd or cream cheese

2 tablespoons icing sugar

Butter, for greasing

6 amaretti, crumbled

Peel the fresh peaches, then cut them in half and remove the stones. If you are using canned peaches, drain them first and pat dry. Put the peaches in a dish, pour the Amaretto over and leave to marinate for 5–10 minutes.

Mix together the mascarpone, curd or cream cheese and icing sugar in a bowl. Cover and chill in the refrigerator until ready to serve.

Heat the grill pan and grease with butter. Remove the peaches from the Amaretto and discard the marinade.

Grill the fresh peaches for 7–10 minutes (4–5 minutes for canned peaches), turning once. Spoon the mascarpone mixture on top of the peaches and serve sprinkled with the amaretti.

27cm Tagine

SERVES 4
Prep time: 10 minutes
Cooking time: 40 minutes

RED PLUMS WITH PINK PEPPERCORNS

A delicious summer treat – ripe plums served with a scoop or two of rich vanilla ice cream.

10 red plums, cut in half and pitted

1 tablespoon olive oil

100g caster sugar

1 teaspoon pink peppercorns, crushed

1 vanilla pod, split lengthways and seeds scraped out

100ml water

Place the plums in the tagine base. Stir in the oil, sugar, pink peppercorns, vanilla seeds and the measured water.

Cover with the lid and poach the plums over a very low heat for 30–40 minutes until soft.

Remove the plums with a slotted spoon and set to one side. Increase the heat to medium and cook the juices in the tagine until reduced and slightly thickened.

Return the plums to the tagine and serve with ice cream.

26cm Round Grill Pan

SERVES 6
Prep time: 10 minutes, plus marinating
Cooking time: 2 minutes

2 tablespoons honey

A few lemon thyme sprigs

Juice of 1 lime

2 tablespoons melted butter

A large pinch of freshly ground
Szechuan pepper

1 cantaloupe melon, cut in half,
deseeded, and each half cut
into 6 slices

GRILLED MELON WITH THYME, HONEY & LIME

A light, fresh and fruity dessert – perfect for hot days.

For the marinade, mix together the honey, lemon thyme, lime juice and melted butter in a large shallow dish until combined. Season with Szechuan pepper.

Add the melon to the dish, spoon over the marinade, cover and leave to marinate in the refrigerator for 1 hour.

Heat the pan over a medium heat. Brush the melon slices with the excess marinade and griddle for 1–2 minutes, turning once, until golden in places.

Serve with thick yogurt or soured cream.

20cm Oval Cast Iron Dish

SERVES 4
Prep time: 15 minutes
Cooking time: 15 minutes

STICKY FRUIT KEBABS

A delicious and colourful way to serve fruit.

½ apple, peeled, cored and cut into equal-sized pieces

Juice of ½ lemon

½ pineapple, skin removed, cored and cut into equal-sized pieces

4 strawberries

4 black grapes

20g butter

1 tablespoon sugar

1 tablespoon honey

Preheat the oven to 175°C.

Sprinkle the apple with the lemon juice to prevent it discolouring. Thread the pineapple, apple, strawberries and grapes onto skewers. (If you are using wooden skewers, soak them for an hour in water before use to prevent them from charring or burning.)

Melt the butter in the ovenproof dish in the oven. Sprinkle the sugar and honey into the dish, mix well and return to the oven for 10 minutes until you have a light caramel.

Remove from the oven and place the fruit kebabs in the dish. Roll the skewers in the caramel until coated.

Turn the oven to a medium-high grill. Place the fruit kebabs under the grill and cook for 2 minutes until starting to colour.

Serve the fruit kebabs with a scoop of vanilla ice cream and a strawberry coulis, if you like.

FLAMBÉED FRUIT WITH SOURED CREAM

Sweet, sour... Divine!

28cm Ceramic Dish

SERVES 4
Prep time: 15 minutes
Cooking time: 20 minutes

25g butter

6 figs, cut in half

3 plums, pitted and cut in half

16 cherries, pitted

50g sugar

40ml Grand Marnier

1 small handful of mint leaves, to decorate

8 tablespoons soured cream or crème fraîche, to serve

Preheat the oven to 200°C.

Grease the ovenproof dish with the butter.

Arrange the figs, plums and cherries in the dish and sprinkle with the sugar.
Place in the oven for 20 minutes until softened.

Remove the dish from the oven and flambé at the table with the Grand Marnier.

Decorate the fruit with the mint leaves and serve with soured cream or crème fraîche on the side.

Round Grill Pan

HONEYED FIG BRUSCHETTA

A sweet bruschetta is an exciting twist on the more usual savoury version.

SERVES 6
Prep time: 10 minutes, plus marinating
Cooking time: 15 minutes

6 tablespoons olive oil

3 tablespoons balsamic vinegar

4 tablespoons honey

12 fresh figs, cut in half

Butter, for spreading

6 slices of bread

Freshly ground black pepper

Chopped mint leaves, to decorate

Soured cream, to serve

Mix together the oil, vinegar and 2 tablespoons of the honey in a bowl until combined. Season with pepper.

Place the figs cut-side down in the dressing, spoon the dressing over and leave them to marinate for 10 minutes, occasionally basting them in the dressing.

Heat the grill pan over a medium heat. Butter the slices of bread and griddle the bread until toasted and golden brown. (You may need to cook them in two batches.) Remove the toasts from the grill and set to one side.

Place the figs in the grill and cook for 3 minutes, turning occasionally, until soft.

Spoon the soured cream onto the grilled toast, followed by the warm figs. Drizzle with the remaining dressing and honey and decorate with mint.

20cm or 22cm Casserole

SERVES 6
Prep time: 10 minutes
Cooking time: 10 minutes

BERRY SOUP
WITH LEMON THYME

**Serve this jewel-coloured fruit 'soup' with a spoonful
of mascarpone and a sprig of fresh mint.**

600g fresh or frozen mixed berries,
including raspberries, redcurrants,
blueberries and strawberries

220ml water, or 50ml if using
frozen fruit

50g soft light brown sugar

1 vanilla pod, split lengthways

Juice of 1 lime

5 lemon thyme sprigs

Prepare the fresh fruit, if using, by removing any stalks or stems and cutting the
strawberries into pieces, if large.

Pour the measured water into the casserole, then add the sugar, vanilla pod, lime
juice and lemon thyme. Stir and cook the fruit over a medium heat for 10 minutes,
or until the sugar dissolves and the fruit is soft.

Keep warm or leave to cool and chill until ready to serve.

To serve, spoon the soup into shallow bowls and top with a spoonful of mascarpone
and a sprinkling of chopped mint.

27cm Tagine

RICE PUDDING WITH LEMON & CINNAMON

A fresh take on a classic favourite.

SERVES 4
Prep time: 10 minutes
Cooking time: 35 minutes

1 litre full-fat milk

Seeds from 1 vanilla pod

1 cinnamon stick

160g pudding rice, rinsed and drained

120g caster sugar

Grated zest of ½ lemon

40g butter, diced

30g unsalted shelled pistachios, chopped

Pour the milk into the tagine base. Add the vanilla seeds and cinnamon to the milk. Bring the milk to a simmer over a medium-low heat.

Add the rice to the milk and return to a simmer.

Reduce the heat to low, cover with the lid and cook for about 30 minutes, or until the rice is cooked. Stir regularly to prevent the rice from catching on the bottom.

Stir the sugar, lemon zest and butter into the rice until combined.

Serve the rice pudding sprinkled with the pistachios.

Square Grill Pan

GRILLED BRIOCHE WITH BRIE, RHUBARB & PISTACHIOS

A delicious variation on traditional French toast.

SERVES 6
Prep time: 5 minutes
Cooking time: 10 minutes

3 eggs

2 tablespoons milk

6 slices of brioche,
cut in half diagonally

20g butter

150g Brie cheese, sliced

1 lemon, cut in half

6 tablespoons rhubarb chutney

4 tablespoons pistachios,
finely chopped

Beat the eggs with the milk in a shallow dish. Dip the slices of brioche into the mixture and drain off any excess.

Heat the grill pan over a medium heat and grease liberally with some of the butter. Griddle the bread on one side until golden brown. Turn the bread over and place a slice of Brie on top and chargrill until golden brown and the cheese has melted slightly. Cook the bread in batches, adding more butter when needed.

Squeeze some lemon juice over the bread and top with a spoonful of rhubarb chutney and a sprinkling of pistachios before serving.

20cm Round Casserole

MAKES: 1 LOAF
Prep time: 25 minutes, plus rising
Cooking time: 40 minutes

BRIOCHE WITH POPPY SEEDS

A delicious enriched loaf with a hint of honey and a poppy seed topping – and it's cooked in a casserole!

700g strong white bread flour, plus extra for dusting

2 teaspoons salt

3 tablespoons poppy seeds

1½ teaspoons (7g sachet) dried yeast

225ml lukewarm water

4 eggs, lightly beaten

2 tablespoons honey

100ml sunflower oil, plus extra for greasing

Mix the flour, salt, 2 tablespoons of the poppy seeds and the dried yeast in a large mixing bowl and make a well in the middle. Add the measured water followed by 3 of the eggs, honey and sunflower oil. Using a large spatula, start to mix the liquid ingredients gently together, then gradually take up the flour, starting in the middle and working your way outwards. Once the mixture has come together into a dough, turn it out onto a well-floured surface.

Knead the dough with well-floured hands for at least 10 minutes until smooth and elastic.

Grease the casserole with a little oil and dust with flour. Place the dough in the casserole, cover with a tea towel and place in a warm, dry place. Leave the dough to rise for 1½ hours, or until it has doubled in size. You can also let it rise in a cool place for a longer period of time.

Preheat the oven to 220°C.

Brush the reserved egg over the risen brioche, then sprinkle the top with the remaining poppy seeds. Bake the brioche for 10 minutes, then reduce the oven to 190°C and continue to bake for a further 30 minutes until risen and golden. Leave to cool slightly in the casserole then turn out and serve warm with butter.

INDEX

An Hachette UK Company
www.hachette.co.uk

First published in Great Britain in 2016
by Mitchell Beazley,
a division of Octopus Publishing Group Ltd
Carmelite House, 50 Victoria Embankment
London EC4Y 0DZ
www.octopusbooks.co.uk

ISBN 978 1 78472 240 1

A CIP catalogue record for this book is available
from the
British Library.

Printed and bound in China

10 9 8 7 6 5 4 3 2 1

Publisher: Alison Starling
Designer: Jaz Bahra
Design: Bold & Noble
Assistant Editor: Ella Parsons
Copy Editor: Nicola Graimes
Senior Production Manager: Katherine Hockley

Standard level spoon measurements are used in
all recipes.
1 tablespoon = one 15 ml spoon
1 teaspoon = one 5 ml spoon

Use fresh herbs, unsalted butter and medium-sized
eggs unless otherwise stated. The Department of
Health advises that eggs should not be consumed
raw. It is prudent for more vulnerable people
such as pregnant and nursing mothers, invalids,
the elderly, babies and young children to avoid
uncooked or lightly cooked dishes with eggs. Once
prepared, these dishes should be kept refrigerated
and used promptly.

Ovens should be preheated to the specific
temperature – if using a fan-assisted oven, follow
manufacturer's instructions for adjusting the time
and the temperature.